Cambridge Elements

Elements in Contentious Politics
edited by
David S. Meyer
University of California, Irvine
Suzanne Staggenborg
University of Pittsburgh

THE TRANSFORMATION OF PROTEST POLITICS

Marco Giugni
University of Geneva

Maria Grasso
Queen Mary University of London

Shaftesbury Road, Cambridge CB2 8EA, United Kingdom

One Liberty Plaza, 20th Floor, New York, NY 10006, USA

477 Williamstown Road, Port Melbourne, VIC 3207, Australia

314–321, 3rd Floor, Plot 3, Splendor Forum, Jasola District Centre, New Delhi – 110025, India

103 Penang Road, #05–06/07, Visioncrest Commercial, Singapore 238467

Cambridge University Press is part of Cambridge University Press & Assessment, a department of the University of Cambridge.

We share the University's mission to contribute to society through the pursuit of education, learning and research at the highest international levels of excellence.

www.cambridge.org
Information on this title: www.cambridge.org/9781009706506

DOI: 10.1017/9781009706490

© Marco Giugni and Maria Grasso 2025

This publication is in copyright. Subject to statutory exception and to the provisions of relevant collective licensing agreements, no reproduction of any part may take place without the written permission of Cambridge University Press & Assessment.

When citing this work, please include a reference to the DOI 10.1017/9781009706490

First published 2025

A catalogue record for this publication is available from the British Library

ISBN 978-1-009-70650-6 Hardback
ISBN 978-1-009-70653-7 Paperback
ISSN 2633-3570 (online)
ISSN 2633-3562 (print)

Cambridge University Press & Assessment has no responsibility for the persistence or accuracy of URLs for external or third-party internet websites referred to in this publication and does not guarantee that any content on such websites is, or will remain, accurate or appropriate.

For EU product safety concerns, contact us at Calle de José Abascal, 56, 1°, 28003 Madrid, Spain, or email eugpsr@cambridge.org

The Transformation of Protest Politics

Elements in Contentious Politics

DOI: 10.1017/9781009706490
First published online: October 2025

Marco Giugni
University of Geneva

Maria Grasso
Queen Mary University of London

Author for correspondence: Marco Giugni, marco.giugni@unige.ch

Abstract: The central questions addressed in this Element are: How has protest politics changed over time, especially but not exclusively in the most recent times? And what are the implications and consequences of these transformations? In this vein, the Element identifies a number of processes of change as outlined in the literature, going from the expansion of the repertoires of contention to the normalization of protest and of the protesters, and the shifting scale of contention to more individual-level processes such as the individualization and digitalization of protest. The Element's aim is to provide a critical discussion of scholarship on the transformation of protest politics and social movement activism.

Keywords: protest politics, expansion, normalization, scale shift, personalization

© Marco Giugni and Maria Grasso 2025

ISBNs: 9781009706506 (HB), 9781009706537 (PB), 9781009706490 (OC)
ISSNs: 2633-3570 (online), 2633-3562 (print)

Contents

1 Introduction   1

2 Expansion: The Broadening of the Repertoires of Contention   6

3 Normalization: The Mainstreaming of Protest Politics   18

4 Scale Shift: From Local to National and Beyond   31

5 Individualization and Digitalization: The Personalization of Protest Politics   37

6 Conclusion   51

References   57

1 Introduction

Protest is not immutable. Quite the contrary, it is a dynamic phenomenon. The most prominent theorization of such a changing character of protest has arguably been offered by Charles Tilly in his analysis of the historical transformation of the repertoires of contention – from an old to a new repertoire – and the related birth of the modern social movement. Despite the importance of Tilly's seminal work on changing repertoires of contention as well as similar efforts to theorize more recent transformations, the changing nature of protest politics has not received the attention it deserves. Scholarship has most often focused on the factors facilitating or preventing the rise of collective action, the internal processes of movement mobilization, and, more recently, on their potential or actual effects. Moreover, at the individual level of analysis, research has overwhelmingly focused on the predictors of activism and protest participation rather than on their transformations.

This Element is entirely devoted to this topic. The central question we address in the pages to follow is: How has protest politics changed over time, especially but not exclusively in the most recent times? In this vein, we identify a number of processes of change as outlined in the literature, going from the expansion of the repertoires of contention to the normalization of protest and protesters and the shifting scale of contention to more individual-level processes such as the personalization of protest. Our aim is to provide a critical discussion of scholarship on the transformation of protest politics and social movement activism. Instead of taking for granted that the processes of transformation discussed in this Element have taken place, we put them under scrutiny, adopting a "healthy skepticism" (Pettigrew 1996) toward our subject matter. By doing so, we hope we can stimulate further research on this topic.

It is important to stress that some of the processes of change discussed in this Element are not restricted to protest politics but bear more broadly on political participation. For this reason, we will widen the discussion where relevant. For example, this is relevant when we discuss the expansion of action repertoires moving beyond forms of protest to embrace new forms and modes of political participation. Similarly, individualization and digitalization are related not only to protest politics but also to political participation more generally. While this will be acknowledged and the discussion extended where relevant, we will focus on how the processes of transformation discussed bear on social movements, protest, and contention.

In this regard, some definition of the contours of our subject matter is in order. Our main focus is on protest politics (henceforth we will mainly use the shorthand protest). Defining protest is not as easy as it could seem at first glance. Some have correctly stressed that this is a fluctuating concept that can vary in meaning (Vassallo 2018). Broadly speaking, "political protest refers to a multitude of methods used by individuals and groups within a political system to express their dissatisfaction with the status quo" (Chong 2015: 421). These include such activities as attending public demonstrations (lawful or illegal), taking part in strikes, and participating in sit-ins, blockades, or other confrontational actions (Giugni and Grasso 2022). Accordingly, protest politics "usually denotes the deliberate and public use of protest by groups or organizations (but rarely individuals) that seek to influence a political decision or process, which they perceive as having negative consequences for themselves, another group or society as a whole" (Rucht 2007: 708).

In fact, there seem to be two approaches in the literature to define protest – or, from an individual point of view, protest participation (Giugni and Grasso 2022). A first, inductive approach starts from a list of specific political activities that are considered unconventional or noninstitutional, such as attending public demonstrations (lawful or illegal), taking part in strikes, and participating in sit-ins, blockades, or other confrontational actions. For example, Barnes and Kaase (1979) famously included in their protest potential scale – which they then crossed with a conventional political scale to create a typology of political action repertoire – the following activities: signing a petition, attending lawful demonstrations, joining boycotts, refusing to pay rent or taxes, occupying buildings or factories, sit-ins, blocking traffic with a street demonstration, and joining wildcat strikes. A second, deductive and more analytical approach consists in defining a number of criteria shared by those activities that we call "protest." In this vein, Dalton (2019) has adapted previous work by Verba et al. (1978) to suggest that protest is characterized as having a high-pressure/high-information type of influence and a collective scope of outcome, being very conflictual, and requiring some or much initiative and cooperation with others.

In an attempt to conceptualize and then empirically confirm different modes of participation, Teorell et al. (2007) proposed a typology of political participation where protest activities reflect an extrarepresentational, voice-based, and nontargeted mode of participation. They then conducted a confirmatory factor analysis to see which specific political activities belong to which mode of participation. Three activities were found to load significantly with the components then interpreted as representing protest activity: take part in a public demonstration, take part in a strike, and participate in illegal protest activities. In a similar, more recent effort, Theocharis and van Deth (2017) found that four items loaded onto the protest component: sign a petition, work for a political action group, join a demonstration, and a residual category of other coded open answers.

Regardless of how it is defined, protest politics is often contrasted to party politics. However, this opposition is not entirely correct, as parties can also engage in protest activities. So it is more a matter of what sorts of activities are conducted than of who carries them out. In an attempt to systematize the matter and locate protest politics within a broader set of related concepts, we suggest distinguishing three other types of politics that may or may not intersect with protest politics depending on how they are defined.

The concept of contentious politics, coined by Charles Tilly in a series of works he began in the 1970s (Tarrow 2014) and further elaborated in particular in two coauthored books (McAdam et al. 2001; Tilly and Tarrow 2015 [2006]), is the one that comes closer to that of protest politics. It refers to "*episodic, public, collective interaction among makers of claims and their objects when: (a) at least one government is a claimant, an object of claims, or a party to the claims, and (b) the claims would, if realized, affect the interests of at least one of the claimants or objects of claims*" (Tarrow 2022: 491; italics in original). This "includes social movements, but it also includes less sustained forms of contention – like riots and strike waves – and more extensive ones – like civil wars, revolutions, and episodes of democratization – and it intersects with routine political processes – like elections and interest group politics" (491). In brief, contentious politics arises from the intersection of three components: contention, politics, and collective action (Tilly and Tarrow 2015 [2006]).

Often the terms "protest politics" and "contentious politics" are used interchangeably. However, we believe that this is not entirely without problems. True, protest politics is highly contentious. But it is also, by definition, collective (to the extent that some prefer to use the term "contentious collective action"; see Goldstone 1998), whereas protest can be understood from both the collective and individual levels. Often, when referring to the individual level, the term "protest participation" (Giugni and Grasso 2022) is used. Yet, at least when it comes to the collective level, protest and contention are close notions.

The concept of lifestyle politics captures another way through which ordinary people may act politically. It is used eminently, if not exclusively, to refer to the individual level. This concept refers to "activities that advance social change by fostering politically inspired lifestyle choices . . ., and as such, they may include various actions carried out within (and beyond) the numerous dimension [*sic*] of everyday life, with different levels of organization, and following very distinct strategic logics" (de Moor 2017: 181; see further Forno and Lorenzini 2022). We will discuss in more detail lifestyle politics later on, as we believe that it marks one of the major processes of transformation we are dealing with here. The main point that we would like to stress at this stage is that lifestyle politics may be considered to some extent as another way to protest.

The fourth and last kind of politics in our conceptual space, routine politics, includes party politics, elections, interest group politics, and other more institutionalized forms of participation and politics. As Tarrow (2022: 491) points out, "[m]uch of politics consists of ceremony, consultation, bureaucratic process, collection of information, registration of events, educational activities, and the like; these actions usually involve little if any collective contention." These and other sorts of routine politics are therefore, by definition, not so contentious, at least not in the sense intended in the contentious politics framework. Yet we conceive of a possible overlap with lifestyle politics insofar as the latter can also be made of routine actions made in one's everyday life.

Protest politics, contentious politics, lifestyle politics, and routine politics may be considered as four basic types of politics that people may engage in. While this Element focuses on protest politics, we will also touch upon issues pertaining to contentious politics and some trespassing into lifestyle politics, while leaving routine politics virtually outside of our framework of discussion as a separate sort of political engagement.

Each of the following sections is devoted to one of four large-scale processes of change. Section 2 deals with the process of expansion – that is, the continued broadening of the repertoires of contention. Since Tilly's seminal work on changing action repertoires, scholars have pointed to the fact that new forms of protest and, more generally, forms and modes of political participation are constantly created by people. This refers not only to large-scale historical processes like those described by Tilly, but also to more recent trends. For example, new social movements and, later on, global justice movements have introduced new ways of protesting in the repertoires of contention. The notion of expansion here is taken in a broad sense, referring both to the "invention" of new ways of protesting and also to the changing meaning of certain existing forms.

Section 3 addresses a well-known process identified by scholars of protest politics: normalization. This refers both to the fact that protest behavior has become increasingly important and legitimate over the years (normalization of protest) and the fact that a broader spectrum of protesters has come to reflect more closely the characteristics of the average citizen (normalization of protesters). This contrasts with the idea of protest being something exceptional carried out by people sharing a specific sociodemographic profile. The first aspect is also reflected in arguments about the rise of a "social movement society" or "protest society," while the second aspect can be understood as "pluralization" of protest politics, meaning that a wide range of different social groups take part in protest activities, or at least in some of them such as street demonstrations. All in all, these changes may be captured through the notion of a mainstreaming of protest politics.

Section 4 refers to the shift of scope of collective action from the local to the national and, more recently, to the transnational level. Social movements often arise at the local level and then shift their scale to the national and sometimes even the transnational level, if and when the circumstances are favorable for such a shift. At the same time, however, one should be cautious of speaking of an inescapable process moving from the local to an "upper" scope. Sometimes a reverse process can be at play, whereby protest activities shift back from the transnational to the national level, for example. The section will discuss these trends, drawing from the literature on scale shift in particular. Different modalities of scale shift will also be discussed.

Section 5 discusses two processes of change that are to some extent related to each other. The first process refers to the increasing individualization of protest politics and of political participation more generally. Particularly the younger generations today often opt for ways of participating that no longer involve engaging in traditional protest activities such as street demonstrations or other forms of protesting, but consist in acting more directly through their personal behaviors in their everyday life. In other words, a shift has occurred from "outward" and public efforts to influence decision-makers or public opinion toward more "inward" and individual forms investing in everyday life and often also bearing on consumption practices. Environment-related activities exemplify this process quite well – for example, through environmentally friendly consumption practices. More generally, this process is captured by the notion of lifestyle politics. In addition, a related process of digitalization of protest politics has occurred, as online forms of protest and, more generally, political participation become more and more frequent and widespread, especially amongst the younger generations. Online activism and digital politics in the context of social movement activism and protest participation is a well-documented phenomenon today. The section will address the extent, causes, and consequences of such a shift from offline to online activism and more generally the transition toward a personalization of protest politics.

The concluding Section 6 first summarizes the main arguments and ideas presented in this Element. Then it discusses directions in which protest politics may be heading, outlining potential scenarios in this regard. Finally, it suggests a number of avenues for further research on the transformation of protest politics to make sense of current and possible future trends.

Before we address in more detail each of the processes of transformation that we have identified, let us say a few more words to clarify the scope of our discussion. While scholarship on protest politics in recent years has indisputably and profitably broadened its attention where it was once mostly – if not entirely – focused on the so-called Western world, our discussion will mainly bear on the latter, most notably Europe and the US. To be sure, we are not claiming that the transformation processes addressed in this Element have not occurred outside of that part of the world, but we focus on those areas where the literature has emerged from and where these processes are most self-evident as trends have matured further in this regard in advanced democracies.

Last but not least, it is worth mentioning that, as will become clear throughout this Element, our discussion to follow owes much to the work of Charles Tilly. Why? For a simple reason: Tilly is no doubt the author who has done the most to show the dynamic nature of social movements, protest, and contention and to study processes of change in the ways in which ordinary people put forth their claims to make themselves heard. That said, our journey into the processes of transformation of protest politics will broadly draw on two major research traditions: from those works in the political participation tradition of political science and political sociology, whereby protest is considered as one mode of engagement amongst others; and works from the tradition of social movement studies, which looks at protest as the principal – though not exclusive – way through which movements make their claims. However, it is worth stressing that, although we will draw profusely from existing scholarly works and hardly lay claim that we are inventing anything new, this is not understood as a literature review but as a focused theoretical work highlighting critical developments for making sense of the evolution of protest to the current historical juncture, so we do not claim exhaustivity in the works cited but rather a focus on the most relevant and salient of these in relation to the transformation of protest politics.

2 Expansion: The Broadening of the Repertoires of Contention

The process we call expansion expresses itself in two movements with both a factual and a cognitive side. On the one hand, it refers to the actual broadening of the repertoires of contention – that is, the means through which ordinary people aim to make their claims heard. On the other hand, it points to the expansion of definitions of political participation and activism as expressed in scholarly work on the matter, but also and perhaps most importantly by the actors themselves. Let us discuss each aspect in turn.

The most authoritative statement about expansion was undoubtedly made by Tilly in his various writings on this topic (see especially Tilly 1986, 1995). His argument is well known: The repertoires of contention – that is, the culturally determined and inevitably limited political means available to citizens at a given time – have undergone a major transformation under the thrust of two large-scale processes, namely capitalism and state formation. These two large-scale processes have created new interests, forms of organizations, and opportunities – in particular at the national level due to the concentration of power implied by state formation – which in turn have led to a major change in the repertoires of contention. Specifically, a repertoire characterized by localized actions, patronized by local elites, and reactive – that is, aiming to preserve existing rights and privileges – was replaced by a national, autonomous, and proactive repertoire. Old forms such as tax revolts, food riots, seizures of grain, and struggles against conscription left the place to new forms such as mass demonstrations, strikes, public rallies, and elections (Tilly 1986). In this perspective, the modern social movement was part and parcel of the new action repertoire and therefore was born in that transformation of action repertoires.

Figure 1 illustrates Tilly's distinction between old and new repertoires of contention based on the two key criteria of scope of action (local vs. national) and orientation – or relation – to power holder (patronized vs. autonomous). Typically, localized and patronized old forms of action such as food riots, seizure of grains, antitax revolts, and other forms of resistance to state expansion were progressively replaced by national and autonomous forms such as petitions, public meetings, mass demonstrations, strikes and, more generally, social movements, and, on the institutional side, elections. This shift from the old to the new action repertoires is aptly summarized as follows by Tarrow (2011 [1994]: 30):

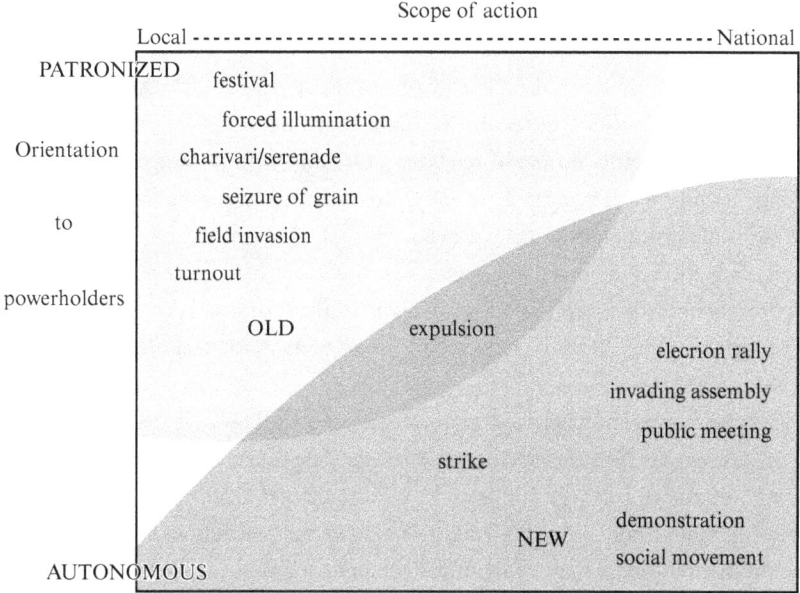

Figure 1 Tilly's old and new repertoires of contention.
Source: Tilly (1986).

> In the 1780s, people knew how to seize shipments of grain, attack tax gatherers, burn tax registers, and take revenge on wrongdoers and people who had violated community norms. But they were not yet familiar with acts like the mass demonstration, the strike, or urban insurrection on behalf of common goals. By the end of the 1848 revolution, the petition, the public meeting, the demonstration, and the barricade were well-known routines, employed for a variety of purposes and by different combinations of social actors.

Tilly's (1986, 1995) theory of changing repertoires of contention is about the modalities through which ordinary people make claims. However, the shift in forms hides a process of expansion in the very content of the claims. While resisting the extraction of resources and conscription – mainly for war-making purposes – was the most common aim of popular uprising in the old repertoire during the ancien régime, the new repertoire also brought about new issues and claims. Table 1 illustrates an effort made to track such a development in Europe beyond the fundamental shift from the old to the new action repertoire (Giugni et al. 2006). This is meant to illustrate in broad strokes the relations between social movements and the state since the seventeenth century, distinguishing between five main historical phases in the development of European society. In this perspective, inspired by Tilly's historical account of contention, each phase is characterized by a central social conflict, a main social movement or movement family, and a type of state and mode of state intervention.

The seventeenth and eighteenth centuries were characterized by the expansion of the national state, whose attempts to rule the population in more direct and intrusive ways spurred various forms of resistance by the ruled. During this period, protest politics reflected the three key features through which Tilly (1986, 1995) described the old repertoire of contention accordingly. The nineteenth century witnessed the consolidation of industrial capitalism, the creation of the proletariat, and the rise of class conflict. As a result, class struggle and poverty came to represent the central conflict that catalyzed protest, and the labor movement became the key movement of that historical period. This marks the shift from the old to the new repertoire of contention, as described by Tilly (1986, 1995).

But the expansion of protest politics did not stop there. At least three subsequent phases can be discerned on this reading. The first is a phase covering more or less the period from the 1900s to the 1960s, characterized by a central conflict pivoting around social rights – and in particular the distribution of welfare – and by the institutionalization of labor movements, but new issues and movements such as peace movements were beginning to come to the fore. The second is a phase from the 1960s to the 1990s, which saw the rise of the new social

Table 1 Phases of development of European society and social movements

Dimensions and periods	Central conflict	Main movements	Type of state and mode of state intervention
Seventeenth and eighteenth centuries	State expansion	Antitax revolts and other forms of resistance to state expansion	Absolutist state; war/direct extraction of human and financial resources
Nineteenth century	Class struggle and poverty	Labor movement	Liberal state; rights, action frame
1900–1960	Distribution of welfare	Institutionalization of the labor movement	Welfare state; planning/ nationalization
1960–1990	Bureaucratization of society and risks linked to economic growth	New social movements	Welfare state; planning/ regulation
Since 1990	Justice and democracy on a global scale	Global justice movements	Multilevel governance; neoliberalism/ loss of control

Source: Adapted from Giugni et al. (2006).

movements mobilizing against the bureaucratization of society and the risks linked to economic growth, but also around emancipatory issues. The third is a phase since the 1990s when issues of justice and democracy on a global scale became increasingly central, with these types of issues raised above all by global justice movements.

An essay outlining this historical reading of the expansion of protest politics in terms of the central social conflicts and the related movements in different periods was published in the mid 2000s. We may therefore wonder whether a new phase has opened since then, with its own features setting it apart from previous epochs. Most notably, we may think of the past two decades as being characterized by a shift from offline to online forms of protesting, under the thrust of the digitalization of society. This could also be related to the emergence of more individualized forms of protest and more generally of political participation. The combined effect of both aspects would be an increasing personalization of politics, which may characterize protest politics in the first part of the twenty-first century. We shall return to this point – including with a critical stance – in particular in Section 5, where we discuss the personalization of protest politics, arguably the most recent process of transformation amongst those we are dealing with here.

All these phases in the broadening and transformation of the action repertoires may be traced back to large-scale processes that have changed society, and therefore also politics at large. The earlier phases, as Tilly (1986, 1995) has shown, are linked to the rise of capitalism and the national state as well as to the related processes of industrialization and urbanization. The post-1960s phase has been associated with the expansion of education and of the welfare state, and the related fundamental value change from materialist to postmaterialist value orientations (Inglehart 1977). Finally, the post-1990s phase may be understood in relation to the process of globalization including the technological revolution brought by the digitalization of society of the so-called knowledge society.

Beyond the simple observation that the forms – but, as we suggested, also the content – of protest have expanded, the question is also why this has occurred. Of course, Tilly has provided his own answer, outlined previously, which fundamentally connects changing action repertoires to the creation of new interests, opportunities, and forms of organization spurred by the two large-scale processes of capitalism and state formation. More generally, proponents of the political process approach to social movements would have a clear-cut answer: This is because conditions change and forms that up until then were effective no longer are. In other words, tactical innovation is linked to changing political opportunity structures. As McAdam (1983: 735) put it, "[l]acking institutionalized power, challengers must devise protest techniques that offset their powerlessness."

Innovating forms of action is one way through which ordinary citizens can make their voices heard (Koopmans 1993), along with the intensity of the event, which may include its size, violence, or duration (Snyder and Kelly 1977). This is something activists know very well. Therefore, if only strategically, they often try to leverage one or more of these factors. However, gathering a large number of people is not always an easy task and requires quite some level of resources, while enacting violent events might go against the principles of a given group or organization and also often has negative repercussions in terms of public image or increased repression from the state. So, in the end, tactical innovation is generally the most viable strategy, although one needs to make use of imagination to continuously find new ways to capture the attention of both public opinion and political authorities.

Examples of innovative forms of action abound. Moreover, some movements have proven quite creative in this regard. Student movements and the new social movements, for example, have introduced some new forms such as street theaters and mock interviews as well as creative and symbolic forms of protest. More recently, the repertoire of contention – of protest but also more generally of political participation – has expanded by also including digital forms, which we discuss in relation to the personalization of protest politics in Section 5. This has brought to the fore other forms of protesting and, more generally, of political participation, such as politically motivated flash mobs, online petitions, and what has come to be known as "slacktivism." Presently, groups of activists such as those from Last Generation have innovated, creating much controversy by throwing paint on artworks in museums or elsewhere, such as in public fountains or other public places. Other recent examples include feminist protesters in costumes inspired by *The Handmaid's Tale*. All this, of course, contributes to broadening the repertoire of contention available to ordinary citizens to protest, in addition to more traditional means such as the petition, the mass demonstration, or the public gathering. To all this, we could add more and more individualized forms of participation consisting in making specific choices in one's own everyday life for ethical or political reasons. We will discuss this aspect further as well in Section 5, including asking whether in this case we can still speak of protest politics or if we rather enter a new domain of engagement.

While, on the one hand, the repertoires of contention expanded with the introduction of new forms, on the other hand, certain forms first took on a different meaning and then were abandoned since they were no longer deemed acceptable or effective. In fact, Tilly's (1986, 1995) theory of changing repertoires discussed earlier illustrates this point precisely. With the structural transformations of European society, certain forms of the old repertoire were no longer helpful and therefore were progressively abandoned. Take for example the *charivari*. This term denotes something that, at least initially, goes beyond politics. Traditionally, "it is the other side of the serenade or aubade, that is, a discordant and thunderous concert, a clash of pots, pans, cauldrons, cornets, possibly accompanied by insults and songs, in front of the home of a person targeted for having broken 'the normal order of things'" (Fureix 2015: 53; our translation from French). In the first part of the nineteenth century, however, the *charivari* started to take on a political meaning as well, particularly in urban spaces (Tilly 1982), and it became part of a repertoire of contention in transformation: "[t]he charivari begins to sanction the transgression of a political norm, to designate an adversary whose delegitimization or even expulsion is sought (rather than reintegration into the community)" (Fureix 2015: 53; our translation from French). As such, this traditional – and eminently local – social rite became a – partly national – political rite with specific political meanings and functions. Once the transition from the old to the new repertoire of contention had been accomplished, however, this form of the *charivari* was progressively abandoned in favor of new forms, most notably that of the street demonstration. Today, the *charivari* – or similar forms – are hardly ever employed. Interestingly, however, some of its elements have reappeared, although somewhat in disguise – for example, as ritual elements within street demonstrations such as those carried out in Argentina in 2001, 2012, and 2015; in Spain in 2004; in Venezuela in 2012; amongst "Quebécquois" students in 2012; or in the "Pots and Pans Revolution" in Iceland in 2009 (Fureix 2015).

Other forms, in contrast, have remained, but their nature has changed. Tax revolts are an example. Fiscal protests still exist today, but the issue became disembodied from the very form of mobilization. The French "yellow vests" of 2018–19 are a recent example of this, at least from what could have been garnered from its initial impetus. Rather than attacking tax gatherers or burning tax registers, as was the case in the old repertoire, they took to the streets – partly peacefully, partly not so – and employed mass demonstrations to protest against the French government's decision to introduce a fuel tax and then against rising fuel prices and the rising costs of living. Austerity protests could be seen as another example, at least in part. While not entirely new from a historical perspective, austerity movements and protests emerged in the wake of the financial and economic crisis of the late 2000s and late 2010s, combining a mix of "old" and "new" issues but with an underlying common goal: that of contesting the negative social and economic consequences of the economic crisis and above all the measures that governments put in place to deal with them such as higher taxes and spending cuts (Grasso and Giugni 2015, 2021). Austerity movements went well beyond fiscal protest, but, even more than global justice movements, they brought questions of redistribution and capitalism back into protest politics (della Porta 2015). As such, issues pertaining to taxation are key to their mobilization, while not the only ones.

Tilly's theory of changing repertoires of contention deals with a transformation that took place long ago, basically in the transition from the ancien régime to the contemporary age. However, the means citizens have at their disposal to make their claims – including those relating to protest politics – have not frozen since. Theocharis and van Deth (2017, 2018) have tried to depict the continuous expansion of the repertoire of political participation since the middle of the twentieth century. Their focus is somewhat different than that of Tilly since they look at various forms of political participation, not only at protest, and moreover they focus on these at the individual level, while Tilly was more interested in collective and contentious forms – that is, contentious politics – although he included elections as part of the new repertoire. Furthermore, and quite significantly, Theocharis and van Deth (2017) stress the fact that the repertoire of participation expanded continuously through the addition of new forms. However, it is less clear whether this also implies the creation of new modes or types of participation, the latter being a set of two or more specific forms that share some features.

In Theocharis and van Deth's (2017) view, reproduced in Figure 2, the development of political participation can be depicted as a continuous process of the rise of new forms that are usually integrated into new modes of participation in broadly and historically defined "waves." Let us quote at some length the authors as they clearly expound their main ideas in their own words:

> As can be seen on this schema, initially, political participation mainly consisted of voting, but new forms associated with representative political institutions (campaigning, contacting officials) established conventional or institutionalized modes of participation. By the end of the 1960s, new forms (demonstrations, sit-ins, signature actions, etc.) expanded the repertoire, adding a protest

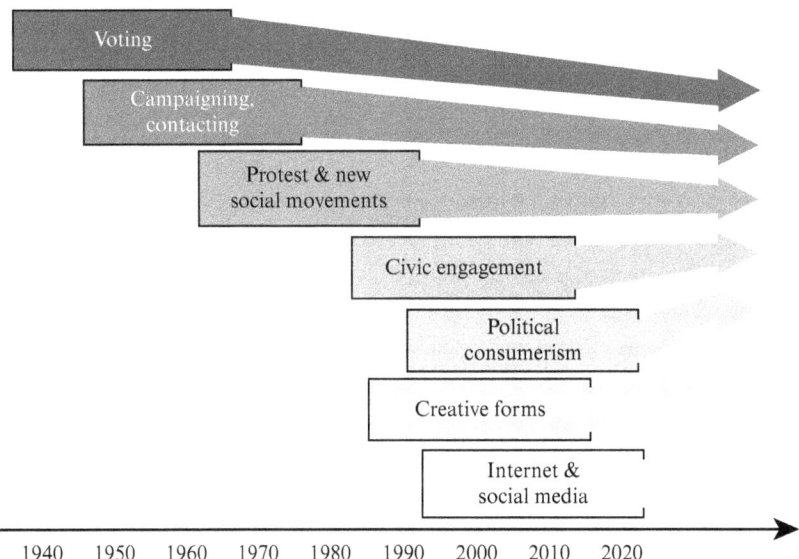

Figure 2 The continuous expansion of the repertoire of political participation since the 1940s.

Source: Theocharis and van Deth (2017).

mode that included acts that were previously perceived as unconventional, but have since gradually become normalized. The same applies for activities by pacifist or women groups that, in the 1970s and '80s, resulted in a mode of political participation related to new social movements. By the early 1990s the gradually disappearing borderline between political and non-political spheres led to the recognition of a new mode of political participation based on civic activities (volunteering, social engagement, working with others to solve local problems, etc.). Some of the recent expansions that became more popular in the new millennium include forms of participation that reflect a more individualistic style of participation and which are characterized by individual lifestyle preferences and a strong emphasis on the expression of moral and ethical standpoints (boycotting, buycotting). The gamut of participatory acts emerging from lifestyle preferences by now includes some of the most imaginative ways of engaging in politics, such as guerrilla gardening, flash mobs and crowd-initiated public assemblies. Finally, the latest addition to the seemingly never-ending expansion of participation includes forms enabled by the internet most prominently social media-such as sharing political content or using social media to mobilize others for political purposes. (Theocharis and van Deth 2017: 18–19)

This process of expansion of the repertoires of contention and political participation can also be seen as a sequence of "waves" that can be situated in time, albeit in an approximate fashion. The first wave – the one described by Tilly (1986, 1995) – occurred, in his view, at the turn of the eighteenth and nineteenth centuries. It was the shift from the old to the new repertoire. The second wave took place with the rise of the new social movements in the aftermath of the 1960s cycle of protest. Together with the student movements of the time, this movement family has largely contributed to innovating – and therefore expanding – the action repertoire of social movements such as, for example, street theatres and other innovative forms of protest action. Supporting this belief, "[s]ocial research has shown that the arrival of the new post-materialistic concerns did not replace the old socio-economic issues, rather they developed alongside them and thus resulted in a general increase in issues generating protest" (Van Alest and Walgrave 2001: 462). The third wave may be situated in the 2000s, when digital means of action became available. The rise of more individualized forms of intervention can arguably be understood as something more continuous, starting with political consumerist practices before the turn of the millennium and leading to lifestyle political practices in the new millennium. As a result of this historical development, today citizens have at their disposal a repertoire made of a still limited but significantly broader number of modes of participation than in previous times. According to these authors, from the 1960s until about the early 2000s, five distinct modes of participation can be identified:

voting, campaign activities, contacting officials or politicians, protest – to which they add new social movements – and social or civic participation.[1]

Theocharis and van Deth's is a valuable and largely agreeable view about how political participation, including protest – has expanded over time. However, some objections can be raised. There is little doubt that forms of participation have expanded during, say, the past century. For sure, certain forms, such as political consumerism and even more so digital forms of participation (these two modes of participation will be discussed in Section 5 as they relate, in our view, to another process of transformation of protest politics) did not exist in earlier times. Yet, it is questionable that protest is something that emerged in the 1960s and 1970s. Forms of protest such as the demonstration, the sit-in and others might have increased in that period – and, as we will see in more detail in Section 3, more as part of a protest cycle than as a long-term trend. However, as Tilly (1986, 1995) has shown they emerged well before. Moreover, adding new social movements to the protest mode is in our view not fully justified. Protest refers to a way to do politics, while the new social movements are a specific movement family that has emerged in that period and made use of various forms of protest as well as other, less contentious forms. As we said earlier, they contributed to renovating the repertoire of contention by introducing some new forms of engagement such as street theaters and mock interviews as well as creative and symbolic forms of protest.

But there is more than "simply" observing whether and when certain forms of protest and, more generally, of political participation have made their appearance. As mentioned earlier, the expansion or transformation of protest politics and more generally of political participation has both a factual and a cognitive side. In other words, this process does not simply refer to "facts" but also to "ideas." It relates to changing conceptions and definitions of what politics is or should be. This is an important aspect that is often overlooked in discussions of protest politics – including ours – which sometimes suffer from a "positivistic" bias whereby what is a form of protest and what does not count as one is decided a priori by the researcher. Similarly, but more broadly, what belongs to political participation and what does not is also something that is set beforehand from an external point of view. Yet scholars have become increasingly sensitive to how ordinary people make sense of politics and what they consider a political act and what not. Of course, one should avoid an "anything-goes" approach that would

---

[1] Once online forms are included, Theocharis and van Deth (2017) identify six modes of participation: voting, institutionalized participation, protest, volunteering, political consumerism, and what they call "digitally networked participation." These modes of participation largely overlap with other typologies, such as, for example, Teorell et al.'s (2007), who distinguished between voting, party activities, consumer participation, protest activity, and contacting.

include everything but the kitchen sink in the definition of political participation, but a perspective that takes into account how people conceive and define what they do may bring fresh air to the field.

In this regard, just as repertoires of contention and political participation have "objectively" expanded, conceptions and definitions of politics have also broadened "subjectively." This is for sure the case when it comes to researchers. Once limited to voting and a handful of other – mainly institutional – forms of action, what is considered political participation and, sometimes, protest, has expanded to include a broader range of activities, from sit-ins to costume parades and pride marches, to hacker attacks to online petitioning and clicktivism. Take for example the mass demonstration. While this form of opposition and resistance has existed at least since the shift from the old to the new repertoire of contention as described by the work of Tilly (1986, 1995), for a long time it was considered as something different from politics, often as an irrational manifestation of a disturbed psychological status, or at a minimum as a nonpolitical reaction to some state of distress or deprivation. This is the underlying assumption of the so-called breakdown or grievance theories of collective behavior, at least in their initial formulations (see Useem 1998 and Buechler 2004 for overviews). In this perspective, the vote is the only and unique legitimate means of expressing political ideas and interests.

This way of thinking, however, was challenged by students of social movements and more specifically by proponents of resource mobilization and political process theories from the 1960s onward. Since then, mass demonstrations and other protest activities have come to be understood as having entered the legitimate repertoire of protest politics, although sometimes we still hear doubts raised with regards to the legitimacy of taking to the streets to express dissent and therefore with regards to the political aims of such activities. In other words, protest was conceived as a rational means to achieve political objectives that could not be obtained by voting or other forms, for example. The fact that many students of social movements were or had been themselves active in social movements and protest groups is not alien to this shift of perspective. Indeed, those researchers could hardly think of themselves as irrational, marginal, and perhaps even "deviant" persons.

Perhaps most importantly in a more "interpretive" approach to the subject matter, we maintain that actors themselves today consider as political acts what in earlier times were not considered as such. Research is lacking in this respect, so we remain cautious and offer this as a hypothesis to be empirically validated or rejected. Yet this hypothesis rests on some existing work showing how people, especially young people, conceive and define politics as well as citizenship (Gamson 1992; O'Toole 2003; Passy and Monsch 2020). If this is true, then the very definition of what constitutes a political act by its own perpetrator may change over time, and we believe that this contributes to the expansion of political participation both within and beyond protest politics. A recent study of young activists in Switzerland, for example, shows that, far from reflecting a prepackaged definition of what is political, they have their own conceptions to which their political activism relates (Holecz 2023).

So protest politics – and politics more generally – has come to invest in other spheres that previously were not considered as political. In particular, certain actions done in one's everyday life may acquire political meaning depending on the motivation given by the author of the act to the very same act. In this vein, Theocharis and van Deth (2017) have not only shown the continuous expansion of the repertoire of political participation as discussed earlier, but also how the very definition of political participation has evolved over time. Perhaps the most significant developments in this respect lie in the inclusion of a whole range of activities and choices made in daily life into the realm of politics. This is connected to what has come to be known as lifestyle politics and the emergence of "self-actualized citizens" (Bennett 2008), especially among the younger generations, which we will discuss in more detail in Section 5 about the personalization of protest politics.

This opens up an important issue that is not directly related to the process of expansion of protest politics but concerns the gendered division between the public (political) and the private (nonpolitical) sphere. Traditionally, the public sphere was considered the prerogative of men, while women were mainly confined to the private sphere and the accomplishment of family tasks. Also thanks to the struggle of feminist movements, this traditional division of tasks was challenged and, slowly, women started to invest in the political sphere as well, both in its institutional – voting – and noninstitutional sides (Grasso and Giugni 2024). For example, women have been found to be more active through informal political efforts and through organizations (Siim 2000; Coffé and Boldenzahl 2010; Stover and Cable 2017). The gender gap has been seen to emerge from a "distinctive processes of social learning and adult roles that centered women in the private domain of the home" (Schlozman et al. 1994: 963). Schlozman et al. (1995: 268) analyzed whether it was the case that "women are more likely than men to anchor their participation in concern for the good of the community; to be active on behalf of issues involving children and families, human welfare, broadly shared interests such as consumer or environmental concerns, and international peace," so that the rise of protest allows an opportunity for studying the new dynamics of gendered political participation. Women have been found to be more likely than men to engage in consumer politics (Acik 2013), sign petitions, or raise money for a social or political group, but however appear to have remained less likely to join a demonstration (Coffé and Bolzendahl 2010). In work examining gendered differences amongst youth to take into account the impact of current socialization dynamics, Grasso and Smith (2022) note how "research has increasingly shown young people's engagement in new social movements and unconventional forms – in many cases particularly amongst young women. Indeed, when we look at these newer modes of engagement young women can actually be seen to be very much politically involved and engaged today."

In sum, concerning the process of expansion, we can conclude that the repertoires of contention have broadened in the course of time. After a major historical shift from an old to a new repertoire as described by the work of Tilly (1986, 1995), which consisted more in a transformation than a proper expansion, the political means available to ordinary people to make their voice heard has continuously expanded in the past century or so. Yet those means remain quite limited in number in the end, although less so than in earlier times. Furthermore, this process of expansion has occurred not only in the forms but also in the issues and claims of movements and protests, witnessing a substantive broadening in addition to the formal one concerning repertoires. Finally, scholarship has also shown that protest politics and, more generally, political participation has expanded because what we consider political today was not seen as such before and politics, once confined to the public sphere, has entered the private sphere as well.

3 Normalization: The Mainstreaming of Protest Politics

One of the most pervasive arguments in the protest politics literature is that protest has not only expanded, but it has also normalized over time, or supposedly so. This is what is usually referred to as normalization. In general terms, this points to the fact that something that once used to be unusual, uncommon, or even exceptional has progressively become normal. But normal may mean different things. When speaking of normalization, the literature means something quite specific that has two sides: the normalization of protest and the normalization of protesters. Let us address in more detail both of these aspects.

To our knowledge, while the idea is arguably older and its seeds lie perhaps in the seminal political action study by Barnes and Kaase (1979), the first explicit statement about the normalization of protest was made by Fuchs (1991) in the early 1990s. This author, in fact, spoke of a "normalization of the unconventional," meaning a normalization of unconventional forms of political participation. He concludes from an analysis of existing survey data that at least since the mid 1970s, a majority of citizens were generally willing to make use of unconventional actions and that such normalization of the unconventional has therefore occurred (Fuchs 1991).

Others have followed suit in subsequent years to show that protest has normalized in the course of time, especially since the emergence of the new social movements and more broadly of the New Left from the late 1960s. This has been identified as the hinge moment when citizens' ways to articulate their interests broadened – for some even shifted – from established channels such as the vote to other, more unconventional forms. Thus, research has pointed to the fact that not only the number of demonstrations, but also the number of people taking part in them has significantly increased in recent decades, while new postmaterialistic concerns have emerged and contributed, alongside older socioeconomic issues, to a general increase in issues generating protest (Van Aelst and Walgrave 2001). Such a greater importance of peaceful protests was accompanied by a greater legitimacy granted to such actions by both citizens and the state, leading to a normalization of protest behavior (Marsh and Kaase 1979; Fuchs 1991; Topf 1995; Van Aelst and Walgrave 2001; Dalton 2008 [1988]). As a result, no longer something unconventional and exceptional, demonstrations have become one of the major channels of public voice and participation in representative democracies (Norris et al. 2005). As Van Alest and Walgrave (2001: 480) have stressed, "Western countries experience almost daily a variety of protest actions and these have become an institutionalised part of the democratic power struggle."

Students of social movements have also pointed to the fact that protest politics has become something "normal" today. We are alluding to the concept of a social movement society (Meyer and Tarrow 1998). In short, in the view of its proponents, it was meant to indicate "that social movements had become ever more common since the 1960s; that this commonality was producing a growing familiarity with protest activity among ordinary people and their rulers; and that this general acceptance was leading – if it had not already led – to the routinization of contention – the rise of a *Social Movement Society* (2011)" (Tarrow, preface to Tilly and Tarrow 2015 [2006]: xi; italics in original). However, as Tarrow admits in the preface to the second edition of his coauthored book *Contentious Politics*, "[o]f these three claims, the first was correct; the second was partly right and partly questionable; and the third was clearly wrong" (xi). The author here seems to be casting doubts on the notion of a social movement society formulated some fifteen years earlier:

> Although routine forms of protest like the public march and the demonstration continued to animate popular politics and to engage broader and broader

sectors of the public, from the turn of the new century more intensive protests appeared in the United States, and more disruptive and more violent forms of contention began to explode across the globe. Not only that: governments – including the American government – were clearly not becoming better accustomed to dealing with protest and were developing more refined and aggressive forms of policing and surveillance. (xi)

This raises a question: Can the thesis of the normalization of protest and the observation that there has been no routinization of contention hold true at the same time? It depends on how we define these terms. We know that normalization implies an increased frequency of use of protest activities – most notably, mass demonstrations – as well as an increased degree of acceptability and legitimacy of the same. This is compatible with the statement that contention has not become routinized, if by the later term we mean something close to what Tilly and Tarrow (2015 [2006]: 62) have called "contained contention" – that is, "contention that takes place within a regime, using its established institutional routines" – as opposed to "transgressive contention," which "challenges these routines and those it protects." As we have mentioned in Section 2, ordinary people continue to innovate and invent new forms and modalities to protest what they believe should be contested, in addition to using more "normal" or "normalized" forms such as the mass demonstration, the public march, or the petition.

As we know, protest is not just a single kind of activity. Quite the contrary, there is a range, albeit limited, of activities people may use to protest against a policy, a legislative measure, or any aspect of the social and political life they consider unjust and needing action to halt or reform. So, an obvious question is: Have all forms of protest normalized? Or is it something we observe more in some forms than in others, or even only in certain forms? The answer is somewhat ambivalent, insofar as scholars tend to speak in general of a "normalization of protest" but then empirical analyses aimed to support that claim often focus on mass demonstrations as the archetypical form of protest politics that has normalized. As such, there is a common understanding that normalization applies more to legal actions and less to illegal protests such as civil disobedience (Fuchs 1991), and more specifically to such actions as the public march and the demonstration.

Some have argued that in addition to a normalization of protest, we have witnessed a parallel process of normalization of protesters, at least to some extent. This could be seen in a broader spectrum of protesters coming to reflect more closely the features of average citizens (Van Aelst and Walgrave 2001). Protest would no longer be confined to the union militants, progressive intellectuals, and committed students as in the past. To use a slogan, "on the street we are all equal" (Van Aelst and Walgrave 2001). According to Van Aelst and Walgrave (2001: 465), such a normalization of protesters can be attributed to two causes: "First, collective action may increasingly involve cross-class collaboration among the population rather than a specific set of social groups. Second, normalisation could result from an increasing number of specific protests being staged by social groups which previously took to the streets only rarely." Moreover, the rise of "emotional mobilizations" is further seen to contribute to normalization.

Elsewhere (Giugni and Grasso 2019, 2022) we used the term "pluralization" to refer to what others have called normalization of protesters. We preferred this term both to mark the distinction with the normalization of protest and because in our view it better conveys the idea that a wider spectrum of people today engage in protest and, more specifically, attend mass demonstrations. Moreover, as we concluded from an analysis of a survey of protesters in seven European countries, pluralization does not refer only to the range of people who participate in protest activities, but also to the mobilization channels though which they get involved and the motives they express for doing so (Giugni and Grasso 2019).

Come to this point, it is worth mentioning an argument that was advanced about people taking part in protest activities and, once again, more specifically in mass demonstrations, as it relates in some way to the normalization of the protesters. This refers to a "homogenization" of protest politics, meaning a rapprochement between two movement families that have characterized much of the contentious space in Europe as well as elsewhere in the past century or so, namely "old" (labor) movements dealing with "material" economic equality, redistribution, and welfare issues, on the one hand, and "new" movements more concerned with "nonmaterial" – or "postmaterial" – cultural and lifestyle issues, on the other (Eggert and Giugni 2012).

Following a skeptical stance vis-à-vis new social movement theory and the extent to which it maintains that these movements are different from older (labor) movements, the argument was advanced that such differences are in fact not – or no longer – so large in the end, resulting in a blurring of the boundaries between "old" and "new" movements and, *in fine*, casting some doubts on this distinction. This argument was then confronted with empirical evidence based on protest survey data, comparing the social composition and value orientations of participants in demonstrations addressing economic and redistributive issues (typical of labor movements) and demonstrations addressing cultural issues (typical of the new social movements). The analyses showed that, in spite of some differences remaining between the two sectors, a – at least partial – blurring of the boundaries between traditional movements and new social movements had occurred, leading, at least to some extent, to a homogenization of the movements of the Left (Eggert and Giugni 2012, 2015; Grasso and Giugni 2015, 2016).[2]

The argument that protest has become more normal today than it used to be in the past, just like the thesis of the normalization of protest applies more forcefully to mass demonstrations, that of the normalization – or pluralization – of protesters can also be seen more specifically in this form of protest. Demonstrations are the most typical form of contentious politics; they are used by different types of people to protest on a variety of issues, and they have become increasingly popular among different social strata (Giugni and Grasso 2019). While they seem to make a more general argument about protest, existing accounts of the normalization of protesters focus on mass demonstrations as the typical form that was normalized (Van Alest and Walgrave 2001; Norris et al. 2005).

While protesters have "normalized," in the sense we just described, we must admit that not everybody takes part in demonstrations, and even less so in other, more radical protest activities. The less well educated, the socially vulnerable, and the needy remain less likely to take to the streets (Van Aelst and Walgrave 2001). Moreover, people with a leftist ideology usually assign a greater importance to protesting in the streets than people with a rightist ideology who tend to privilege more institutional channels (Kriesi 1999). These different attitudes vis-à-vis protest politics reflect a cultural difference between the left and the right. People on the left tend to stress more direct, bottom-up and participatory forms of democracy, whereas people on the right usually prioritize top-down intervention and representative democracy (della Porta 1996). Thus we could say that normalization is not for everybody, whether this results from a lack of resources by some or a deliberate choice not to engage in certain forms of activism.

But what empirical evidence do we have to prove that both a normalization of protest and a normalization of protesters have occurred? Concerning the normalization of protest, this can be done from a collective or an individual perspective. Concerning the former, we may look at the development over time of protest actions carried out by social movements, or other actors for that matter. A now standard method amongst students of social movements to do so is to carry out a protest event analysis, consisting in tracking protest actions over time in a public record source – most often newspapers – in

---

[2] Elsewhere Giugni and Grasso (2019, 2020) we referred to such "homogenization" across movement sectors as a further possible process of change. Here, however, we decided not to treat this as a process of transformation of protest politics on an equal footing with the others, because this is a more specific and speculative kind of process, not so widespread in the literature as the other ones.

a systematic manner (see Koopmans and Rucht 2002 and Hutter 2014a for discussions of the method).

Van Alest and Walgrave (2001) show protest event data for Belgium showing that both the number of demonstrations and that of demonstrators have risen steadily in Belgium since the 1950s. Moreover, they refer to Rucht (1998) pointing to a similar, albeit less linear trend in Germany. As Tarrow (2011 [1994]) as well as others have maintained, however, protest follows ebbs and flows, due among other things to the opening up or closing down of political opportunities – so-called windows of opportunity – and often occurs as cycles or waves of contention rather than displaying a regular – upward or downward – trend. This makes it hard to confront the thesis of the normalization of protest according to this criterion. To do so, we would need data over a longer period than a few years to try to discern a trend behind such ebbs and flows. For example, Tarrow (1989) has studied the Italian cycle of contention of the years 1965–75 in Italy. Similarly, in one of the first systematic comparative studies based on protest event analysis, Kriesi et al. (1995) have shown that levels of protest not only vary across countries depending on the availability of opportunities, but also over time in a relatively trendless manner. In a similar fashion, Hutter (2014b) extended Kriesi et al.'s (1995) study and data set to show how major new cleavages restructured protest politics over a thirty-year period. More recently, Kriesi et al. (2020), arguably in the most comprehensive overview of the waves of protest mobilization that spread across Europe to date, show data encompassing the years from 2000 to 2015 and covering a broader range of thirty countries.

All these as well as other existing protest event datasets show that the most striking feature of protest is not necessarily a systematic increase but rather the adaptation of protesters to their broader environment and the consequent wavelike pattern of protest activities as well as the strong cross-country variations in those activities. If we take for example the most extended and broader dataset – the one by Kriesi et al. (2020) – if any, we observe a declining trend as the number of events in their sample go from a highest level of 2,586 in 2000 down to a lowest level of 1,297 in 2014 and then 1,503 in 2015.[3] However, protests went already down to 1,478 in 2004 and then up again to 2,473 in 2008. So the difference between the start and the end of the period considered is better interpreted in our view as part of a cyclical pattern typical of protest politics rather than a sign of a systematic trend.

A similar wavelike pattern can be observed for protest by the far right (Castelli Gattinara et al. 2022).[4] An analysis of quarterly rates of protest events

---

[3] Our analysis of original data. Source: https://poldem.eui.eu.
[4] Available infographics. Source: https://farpo.eu.

by this family of political actors – still an understudied kind of movement and protest – from 2008 to 2021 shows ups and downs as well as important cross-national differences, and it is hard to discern any systematic upward or downward trend. Once again, waves or cycles rather than trends seem to better represent what is going on.

One could also look at specific forms, such as strikes, of which systematic longitudinal data exist, in addition to those we can extract from protest event sources. Once again, for this specific form of protest, it is hard to discern a rising trend in labor unrest, whether in terms of frequency, size, or duration of strikes. It is more a matter of ups and downs depending on a number of factors such as, for example, shifts in the political position of labor in the national power (Shorter and Tilly 1974). Therefore, the most striking fact is that there are stronger differences across countries than over time. If any, in the long run, there is a declining trend of strike activity and industrial unionism (Visser 2012) a bit everywhere rather than an increase (Bordogna 2010), above and beyond cyclical fluctuations that typically characterize strike activity (Franzosi 2023).

But there is a second problem with the use of protest event data or other measures of protest activity to assess the normalization thesis: the lack of a reference line. In other words, showing that protest actions have increased over time is not a strong test as we do not know what happens with other forms of politics. Perhaps other forms have also increased, so that in the end we would not know whether we witness a normalization of protest rather than a "normalization of politics," at least of "public" politics, meaning a rise in people's political engagement in overt political activities overall. So the indicator is not the absolute level of protests but rather the share of protests over a hypothetical total of political activities. This would require tracking protest actions but also other forms of politics. Unfortunately, to our knowledge there is no general dataset allowing for this kind of analysis. The closest we can get to doing this kind of analysis is by looking at so-called claims-making data, a kind of data that can be considered as an extension of protest event data but covering verbal statements in addition to protest actions and including all types of actors rather than limiting to social movement actors (Koopmans and Statham 1999). In this way, one has a baseline against which to assess the observed increase or decrease in protest actions. The ratio between protest actions and verbal forms of political interventions in the public domain is arguably only a rough indicator of the importance of protest at a given point in time, but it is a better one as compared to the mere absolute number of protest events.

Just as protest event datasets are limited in time and territorial scope – although comparative datasets have become more frequent over time – claims-making datasets are also limited and less widespread and, moreover, deal with a specific political or policy field such as the field of immigration and ethnic relations politics (Koopmans et al. 2005), the field of unemployment politics (Giugni 2010), or a specific topic or issue such as Islam (Cinalli and Giugni 2013), the economic crisis (Cinalli and Giugni 2016) or youth politics (Kousis and Giugni 2020), just to mention some projects in which one of the present authors was involved. For example, data reported in Cinalli and Giugni (2016) in relation to the economic crisis shows trendless fluctuation between 3 and 7 percent from 2008 to 2014. Therefore, existing claims-making datasets would at best give us a partial view – and above all, one that is limited in time – about a possible increase of protest actions as compared to other, verbal forms. What is certain is that, over all forms of strategic interventions in the public domain – the definition of what a claim is – only a minor part is represented by protest actions. This suggests, once again, that mass demonstrations, and even less so other forms of protest, are more "normal" today that they used to be in the past but they are far from being something routinely done by all citizens.

Having established that available protest event or claims-making data can hardly give us a definitive answer about the normalization of protest, another way to assess the normalization thesis consists in examining whether protest, as a specific individual mode of political participation, has become more frequent over time. Here one can use various existing comparative datasets, such as the European Social Survey (ESS), the European Value Survey (EVS), or the World Value Survey (WVS), which track characteristics, opinions, and attitudes of citizens in a number of countries included in the data. Electoral studies data can also be used, but usually they are limited to a single country, so that one needs to repeat the analysis for each single country to get a broader, comparative picture. Finally, there are some ad hoc datasets created by teams of researchers for specific purposes but that, if made available, may be reanalyzed for this aim.

Van Aelst and Walgrave (2001) show evidence based on such existing survey data that seem to support the thesis of a normalization of protest. They show that in all the six Western countries included in the political action study (Barnes and Kaase 1979) the share of people who said they attended lawful demonstrations increased significantly from 1981 to 1990. Moreover, for the three countries for which data exist for that year, the increase started already in 1974.

Our own analysis of existing survey data provides additional evidence on a broader range of political activities. Table 2 shows this indicator in eight.[5] European countries for the 1981–2021 period based on the EVS trend data. We use these data instead of the ESS as this latter covers a shorter period of time, starting only in 2002. The question asked whether the respondents had already

---

[5] Britain, Denmark, France, Germany, Italy, Netherlands, Spain, and Sweden.

Table 2 Use of five political activities in eight European countries from 1981 to 2021 (percentages)

	1981–1984	1990–1993	1999–2001	2008–2010	2017–2021
Signing a petition	42.5	53.3	60.5	59.9	58.1
Joining in boycotts	8.3	9.8	15.3	13.5	15.7
Attending lawful/peaceful demonstrations	19.4	27.9	31.9	30.8	31.1
Joining unofficial strikes	5.3	6.2	7.9	7.8	9.8
Occupying buildings or factories	3.2	3.1	4.6	3.8	-

Source: EVS Trend File 1981–2017 (https://search.gesis.org/research_data/ZA7503).

done in the past, might be willing to do, or would never do the following political activities: signing a petition, joining in boycotts, attending lawful/peaceful demonstrations – the kind of activity that interests us the most here – joining unofficial strikes, or occupying buildings or factories (here we only show the "have done" measure). These are all activities that might be included in what we call protest politics, although signing petitions and joining in boycotts are sometimes perhaps better conceptualized as political consumerist activities – that is, as part of another mode of participation, also based on a factor analysis of political activities (Teorell et al. 2007).

For all these political activities but one, the trend is quite clear and consistent: Whether it is about signing a petition, joining a boycott, attending a demonstration, or joining a strike, the numbers show an increase overall. The only exception to this trend is more radical actions such as occupying buildings or factories, which have remained quite stable over time and at a much lower level. Such an increase meets the expectations of the normalization thesis, at least for what concerns the frequency at which people adopt protest activities. At the same time, however, at some point the increase flattens out. Specifically, the rise in the use of extra-institutional political activities concerns above all the first three survey waves (1981–4, 1990–3, and 1999–2001), while from the late 1990s or early 2000s we observe a more stable trend. This might suggest, on the one hand, that the process of normalization started well before the early 1980s, when the first available survey wave was carried out. On the other hand, and related, protest participation – at least in the forms at hand – might have reached a sort of ceiling whereby the share of people participating in these political activities can hardly increase further unless something is done in terms of reducing the inequalities in protest participation and more generally in political participation.

This is the situation in Europe, which is the focus of our discussion. But how about in other regions? Perhaps protest politics – and, more specifically, mass demonstrations – has normalized in Europe but not yet in other parts of the world. To ascertain this, we can take a look at time series data provided by Quaranta (2017) for a specific yet fundamental form of participation. He shows long-terms developments of attendance to lawful demonstrations in four groups of countries between 1981 and 2014, also using EVS/WVS data. These data give us a more nuanced and complex picture suggesting that the normalization of protest is perhaps not a general and even less so a universal process, at least from the early 1980s onward. Rather, trends differ across single countries as well as across groups of countries. In most cases, the data overall show either a stable or fluctuating trend. This holds for the advanced democracies (Denmark, France, Germany, Great Britain, and the United States), Latin American countries (Argentina, Brazil, Chile, Mexico, Peru, and Uruguay), and the group of other countries (India, Nigeria, Philippines, South Africa, South Korea, and Turkey). Especially among the advanced democracies, some specific countries display an increase in protest participation while others show a slight decrease, but it is hard to discern an overall pattern suggesting an upward trend that applies everywhere. Things, however, are much different for the group of postcommunist countries (Czech Republic, Latvia, Romania, Russian Federation, Slovenia, and Ukraine). There we observe an overall declining trend from 1990 onward, perhaps except in Slovenia. So protest participation, if any – at least as measured through attendance in lawful demonstrations – has remained quite stable or even declined in certain contexts. Such a decline may be due to a variety of reasons. These may have to do with specific developments in those countries that display a declining trend, for example in terms of changing political opportunities or still other factors. It may also be due to shifting repertoires, for example to the rise of online protest activism, which could have partly substituted the more traditional offline activities. We shall return to this aspect in Section 5.

Thus, we have mixed evidence about the normalization of protest. Our own analysis of different political activities shows a clear rising pattern up until a certain moment, followed by stability. Other data on mass demonstrations, however, suggest that the picture is more nuanced and complex, with different trends across regions – some supporting the normalization thesis and others not – as well as across specific countries But a "normalized" form of action is not only one that is more frequently used than in the past; it is also one that has become more accepted and legitimate. So a further way to confront the thesis of the normalization of protest, again at the individual level of analysis, would be by ascertaining whether people believe that protest has become more acceptable as a way to do politics than it was in the past. In this regard, Van Aelst and Walgrave (2001) refer to a number of studies showing that lawful demonstrations are becoming increasingly accepted (Marsh 1977) and that both the number and legitimacy of peaceful – the qualification is important – demonstrations have increased considerably in Western Europe (Fuchs 1991; Topf 1995). They also report some numbers further supporting this claim: for example that, in France, the share of people who approved strongly of lawful demonstration as a form of protest went from 50 percent in 1988 to 62 percent in 1995 (Favre et al. 1997); or that, in Belgium, this share was already 75 percent in 1995 (Beerten et al. 1997). They add that "[t]hese results contrast sharply with figures on more obstructive and violent acts" (Van Aelst and Walgrave 2001: 464). Based on these as well as other examples, they "conclude that that the growing number of peaceful protests and the increased legitimacy accorded to such actions support traditional theories of the normalisation of protest behaviour" (464). Unfortunately, general repeated cross-national surveys such as the ESS, the EVS, or the WVS do not include measures of these aspects allowing us to do our own analysis.

Turning to the empirical assessment of the second part of the normalization thesis – that is, the normalization of protesters, or pluralization – one way to do so consists in looking at who participates in protest activities and, more specifically, in mass demonstrations. Norris et al. (2005) as well as Van Aelst and Walgrave (2001), in fact, have provided some evidence supporting the thesis of a normalization of the protesters examining whether they are indeed made up of individuals that resemble in makeup the general population or not. In both studies, however, the analysis is limited to a specific national case, namely Belgium where suitable data were available. Since we know, and the authors admit themselves, that the context matters much when it comes to protest politics, we may wonder whether these findings can be generalized. In this regard, our own analysis based on protest survey data in seven European countries also suggests that street demonstrations have become more "plural" in terms of the range of people participating, channels of recruitment – including now both offline and online channels – issues addressed, and motives of participants (Giugni and Grasso 2019). Protest surveys allow us to survey protesters "in the act" and therefore to study in detail their characteristics, for example in comparing novice with repeat protesters (Klandermans et al. 2014).

Just as we have done for the normalization of protest, we may look at existing survey data to ascertain the normalization of the protesters. Ultimately, the thesis of the normalization of protesters rests on two assumptions: first, that a wider range of people today participate in protest activities, most notably mass demonstrations, than used to be the case earlier in time; and second, that the difference between those who protest and those who do not is shrinking. The first implication means that the social composition of protests has become more heterogeneous, while the second means that protesters no longer have a specific social profile, or at least a much less different from that of nonprotesters. Table 3 shows, based on EVS/WVS data, the sociodemographic background of people participating in protest activities in eight European countries for the 1981–2021 period based on the EVS trend data. It shows whether and how the social profile of protesters, as opposed to nonprotesters, has changed over time, specifically in terms of age, gender, education, employment status, and occupational class.

Generally speaking, we observe a rise in protest participation on all counts and for all groups. Concerning gender, whereas in the early 1980s, men used to protest much more often than women – attesting to a strong gender gap in

Table 3 Who protests? Participants in protest activities in eight European countries from 1981 to 2021 (percentages)

	1981–1984	1990–1993	1999–2001	2008–2010	2017–2021
Gender					
Female	14.0	23.4	28.1	29.6	30.0
Male	25.1	32.7	36.0	32.0	32.3
Age					
18–34	26.9	33.9	33.4	32.6	29.4
35–59	15.9	29.2	35.9	34.4	33.7
60+	9.4	14.3	23.4	24.5	29.3
Education					
High (completed 19+ years)	30.3	39.5	44.7	40.5	37.3
Low (completed 18 or fewer years)	13.8	21.6	24.5	23.9	23.3
Occupational class					
Manual	17.8	25.6	28.0	24.7	23.8
Nonmanual	22.0	29.8	36.3	33.5	33.9
Employment status					
Unemployed	27.2	26.8	35.4	26.8	29.2
Employed full-time	24.3	35.0	36.6	36.2	33.5

Source: EVS Trend File 1981–2017 (https://search.gesis.org/research_data/ZA7503).

protest participation paralleling that in other modes of participation such as voting – in the late 2000s, the gap virtually closed up, especially thanks to the much greater participation of women. A similar trend can be seen for age: There is an increase for all three age groups, but especially so for the middle-age group as well as for the older cohorts. So, while in 1981–4, protesters were largely made of young people under thirty-five, in 2017–21, this was no longer true and they are more evenly distributed across age groups and protest therefore involves broader segments of the population.

Thus the data provide evidence for a normalization of the protesters in terms of gender and age, at least for the countries included here. We can draw a similar conclusion also for education and occupation. An important gap in education – the more educated protest more – remains, but both those with a higher and those with a lower level of education are more involved in protest activities in the more recent years. Further, both manual and nonmanual occupations have become more often involved in protests in time. In this case, however, the gap between the two occupational classes has widened, suggesting that the normalization of protesters may also lead to political inequality in some ways. Finally, both unemployed and full-time employed people protest more in the more recent period than they used to do about four decades earlier. This holds above all for the latter, so much that the gap has reversed: In recent times, employed people protest more than unemployed people, suggesting that protest is not – or no longer – a tool of the most deprived but has become a form of politics that may be done by everyone, even though not everyone does it in the end.

In sum, concerning the process of normalization, there is evidence that protest politics has normalized, both in terms of a greater acceptance and legitimacy of certain forms of protest such as in particular mass demonstrations and in terms of the profile of those who take part in such political activities. This process is arguably something that occurred already quite a while ago, whereas it is hard to observe a general rise in protest activities – in particular, mass demonstrations – in the more recent decades. If any, there is a stable or in some case even a declining trend. Furthermore, there are limits to normalization. On the one hand, it does not concern more confrontational or even illegal actions, let alone violent ones, and even for the more mainstream forms the increase in their use seems to have capped. On the other hand, participation in mass demonstrations – the archetypical normalized form of protest – remains more accessible to those who have more resources, while the resource-poor – the less well educated, the socially vulnerable, and the needy – are less likely to resort to protest and remain less likely to take to the streets.

4 Scale Shift: From Local to National and Beyond

The work by Tilly (1986, 1995) about changing repertoires of contention is focused particularly on the next process of transformation we think it is important to address: scale shift. Broadly speaking, scale shift refers to the fact that protest politics has changed its scope. In his seminal work, Tilly has masterfully shown how contention has historically moved from local settings to national scope, in addition to becoming more autonomous and proactive. So, in a way, his theory about changing action repertoires is also a theory about scale shift.

But scale shift among social movement scholars, at least recently, has mainly referred to the changing scope from the national to the transnational level. How many times have we heard in the past two or three decades that the world is increasingly globalized? Parallel to the rise of scholarly works on globalization and its effects on various aspects of social and political life, research has paid increasing attention to such a transnational dimension of protest politics, particularly with reference to social movements that acquire a scope that goes beyond the local or national one. This shift – or, more accurately, scaling up – of attention occurred according to the social movement literature in the late 1990s and early 2000s, often in relation to the rise and mobilization of global justice movements (della Porta et al. 1999, 2006; Smith and Johnston 2002; Pianta 2004; della Porta and Tarrow 2005; Tarrow 2005). As such, scholars have asked about the "transnational condition" in relation to protest politics (Teune 2010). More broadly, a whole strand of literature has emerged, pointing to the fact that the development of transnational networks and movements indicates the emergence of a global civil society – a concept popular especially in the field of international relations – surpassing the traditional national context for mobilization (Kaldor 2003).

The whole contentious politics agenda has paid much attention to the broadening of the scope of contention from the national to the transnational level. Indeed, in a programmatic article published in the very first issue of the journal *Mobilization*, which would a few years later take on increasing substance in two important books (McAdam et al. 2001; Tilly and Tarrow 2015 [2006]), McAdam et al. (1996: 19) aimed, among other things, "to give serious thought to how the forms and dynamics of popular protest are changing in the context of what some have called the age of 'globalization.'"

In McAdam et al.'s (2001) perspective, scale shift refers to something more than a simple shift of protest politics from the national to the transnational level. It forms one of the "robust processes" they identified – along with actor constitution and polarization, and later on still others – that account for the spread of contention from one specific locality to a broader setting. In this perspective, the process of scale shift can be seen in broad terms as leading to coordinated action and therefore also to the creation of social movements – that is, if we follow the idea that social movements are specific modes of coordination of collective action, one characterized by a combination of intense resource exchanges and boundary work at field level (Diani 2015).

Much of the scholarly discussion about scale shift, however, has dealt more specifically with the transnationalization of social movements. This occurred especially in the first half of the first decade of the new millennium, when the rise of global justice movements as well as other movements mobilizing beyond the national borders attracted the attention of many analysts, both among students of social movements and scholars in research strands in international relations. In this perspective, scholars have stressed that there is no single process of scale shift of protest politics to the transnational level. For example, della Porta and Tarrow (2005) distinguish between four types of transnationalization in relation to social movements and contention: diffusion, domestication (or internalization), externalization, and transnational collective action (see further Balme and Chabanet 2002 as well as della Porta and Caiani 2011 for similar efforts with specific reference to the Europeanization of protest). Here is how they define them: "By *diffusion*, we mean the spread of movement ideas, practices, and frames from one country to another; by *domestication*, we mean the playing out on domestic territory of conflicts that have their origin externally; and by *externalization*, we mean the challenge to supranational institutions to intervene in domestic problems or conflicts" (della Porta and Tarrow 2005: 2; italics in original). The fourth type is called transnational collective action, defined as "*coordinated international campaigns on the part of networks of activists against international actors, other states, or international institutions*" (della Porta and Tarrow 2005: 2–3; italics in original). While the first three processes are both as important and widespread, this fourth process is seen as a "new transnational activism" (Tarrow 2005) – perhaps an even more "genuine" one – as most notably exemplified by the emergence and mobilization of global justice movements in the late 1990s and early 2000s.

In a somewhat similar fashion, but at the same time broadening the perspective, Tarrow (2005) mentions six processes of transnational contention, reflecting different ways in which activists approach internationalism to pursue their interests. These are global framing, internalization, diffusion, scale shift, externalization, and coalition forming. As we can see, four of these processes are those evoked earlier in this Element (scale shift corresponds to transnational collective action), but they are supplemented by global framing (the creation of collective action frames at the global level) and coalition forming (the creation of transnational coalitions).

All these taxonomies and typologies have a descriptive aim. As such, they are meant to show that there are multiple ways in which protest politics may go beyond the national borders. This is itself an important point, as we started this section with a generic statement about the fact that protest politics has shifted its scope from the local, first to the national and then to the transnational or supranational level. Yet these are more than simple descriptive concepts. In a way, they are also explanatory concepts, insofar as they suggest ways in which protest may move from the local up to the national and especially transnational level.

Such an explanatory – mechanism-based – perspective is at the heart of McAdam et al.'s (2001) endeavor. Specifically, how does scale shift – whether from the local to the national or up to the transnational level – occur? McAdam et al. (2001) suggested that the scaling up from localized action to coordinated action may follow two channels: a direct channel in which a broker – a social movement organization or other – establishes a link between a local actor and activities to other actors and localities, and a mediated channel acting through a logic of diffusion. These are seen as two distinct mechanisms through which scale shift may take place. Both mechanisms work insofar as some kind of attribution of similarity (see further McAdam and Ruch 1993) may be activated, which in turn leads to emulation of action and therefore to a scale shift.

An important aspect in discussions about the scale shift of protest politics, in particular from the national to the transnational level, concerns the extent to which national political opportunities still influence and channel movements and protests in the era of globalization. Two views can be discerned in this regard. They reflect existing views about globalization. On the one hand, an "optimistic" stance, often borrowed from the "global civil society" thesis (Kaldor 2003), maintains that globalization and the related denationalization have eroded much if not all the power of national states and therefore their structuring role vis-à-vis social movements (Chase-Dunn and Almeida 2020; see Almeida and Chase-Dunn 2018 for an overview). On the other hand, a more "skeptical" stance, while not rejecting the obvious observation that the world has become more global and that, consequently, national and constraints are now flanked at least in part by supranational ones, argues that they continue to exert an important influence on movements and protests (Tarrow 2001, 2005; della Porta and Tarrow 2005; Giugni et al. 2006, 2010). As such, transnational contention resembles more what Tarrow (2005) has called "complex transnationalism," a system "in which states, international institutions, and nonstate actors regularly interact around issues of global importance" (della Porta and Tarrow 2005: 17).

The idea that national opportunities and constraints remain important even in an era of increasing transnationalization of contention is reflected at the individual level by the notion of "rooted cosmopolitans" (Tarrow 2005, 2012). This notion refers to *"individuals and groups who mobilize domestic and international resources and opportunities to advance claims on behalf of external actors, against external opponents, or in favor of goals they hold in common with transnational allies"* (Tarrow 2005: 29; italics in original). Transnational activists, in this view, are a specific type of such rooted cosmopolitans and can be defined as *"people and groups who are rooted in specific national contexts, but who engage in contentious political activities that involve them in transnational networks of contacts and conflicts"* (Tarrow 2005: 29; italics in original). The important point here is that, even if they engage in transnational protest and other activities, transnational activists do not come out of the blue, but remain closely linked to domestic networks and opportunities.

But, when it comes to empirical evidence, are we witnessing an actual shift from the national to the transnational level – or from the local level, for that matter – which has occurred and is still occurring? Or is it simply the result of a shift in attention paid by scholars to transnational protests and movements? A number of authors have tried to answer this question, at least for what concerns the European level. Indeed, parallel to the rise of scholarly works on transnational contention, a relatively small but significant body of literature has focused on the process of Europeanization of protest (Uwe 1998; Imig 2002; della Porta and Caiani 2011; Dolezal and Hutter 2012). These works go back to the early 2000s, but for the most part they provide only limited evidence of a process of Europeanization of collective action. Imig and Tarrow (2001), for example, have asked a number of questions relating to the consequences of the process of European integration for contentious politics and especially for social movements. The most important for our present purpose is the following: Is the process of European integration shifting the targets of social movements from the national arena to the European Union level? They base their analysis on a longitudinal and cross-national dataset on contentious political action.

While the emergence of a supranational realm of European government offers new opportunities and constraints for domestic social actors, the barriers to launching contentious action in Europe remains very high for social movements. So, at least at the time they wrote, the Europeanization of contention remained a marginal process, with only a little less than 500 protest actions over a total of nearly 9,900 they found during the 1984–97 period. This, incidentally, contrasts a great deal with what happened to interest groups, whose activities in Brussels have continued to grow over time (Balme and Chabanet 2008). Clearly, Europeanization favors strongly organized, professionalized, and

The Transformation of Protest Politics

more powerful organizations that better adapt to the logic of European bureaucratic institutions, while grassroots, social-movement-like ones are less able to seize those opportunities opening up at that level, and when they do so their ultimate goal is often to get leverage over national-level actors and institutions by addressing international ones (Keck and Sikkink 1998; della Porta and Tarrow 2005).

Rucht (2002) has also inquired into the process of Europeanization of collective action using empirical evidence made of protest event data, coming to similar conclusions. His analysis focuses on one specific country, namely Germany. He looked in particular at the territorial level of mobilization, the territorial scope of the problem addressed in the protest, and the territorial level of the targets of the protest. He concluded quite bluntly that "[t]aken together, the data presented in this section convey a clear message. As far as Germany is concerned, the Europeanisation and, more generally, internationalisation of protest is a myth. Europeanisation does not even occur in the area of environmental mobilisation, which, one might assume, would clearly exhibit such a tendency" (Rucht 2002: 46).

Following the path traced by these authors, we can exploit a protest event dataset on six European countries from 1975 to 2011 to examine the extent to which protests have taken on an increasing supranational character.[6] Table 4 shows the distribution of these protest events according to the administrative-territorial level of their addressee. The events have been grouped in five-year periods for ease of reading. As we can see, it is hard to discern a trend in these data. For sure we cannot speak of a trend toward an increasing internationalization or transnationalization of protests. Protests with an international character were more frequent after 2000 than before 1985, but then went down again in the last two years covered by the data. Also, a peak in international events occurred already in the second half of the 1980s.

So, rather than a trend pointing to an increasing international or transnational character of protest politics, what we observe are ups and downs in this respect. On the other hand, national targets remain by and large predominant throughout the entire period. This joins the conclusions by Imig and Tarrow (2001), Rucht (2002), and still others about the fact that contention – at least it was up until the period covered by the data – is far from having shifted the scale from the national to the transnational level. A similar observation has been made about claims making in the field of immigration and ethnic relations politics, for example (Koopmans et al. 2005), a field where talks about denationalization

---

[6] Austria, Great Britain, France, Germany, Netherlands, and Switzerland. The data about France only cover the 1975–2005 period.

Table 4 Level of addressee of protest events in six European countries from 1975 to 2011 (percentages)

	1975–1979	1980–1984	1985–1989	1990–1994	1995–1999	2000–2004	2005–2009	2010–2011
International (incl. European)	11.9	12.5	19.9	13.7	16.7	19.9	19.8	13.3
National	60.5	47.3	51.2	71.1	73.1	72.8	70.9	77.8
Subnational (regional or local)	27.7	40.2	29.0	15.2	10.1	7.3	9.2	8.8
Total	100%	100%	100%	100%	100%	100%	100%	100%
N	2,336	3,375	2,625	3,285	3503	2,470	1524	622

Source: Observatory for Political Conflict and Democracy in Europe (https://poldem.eui.eu).

and "postnational" citizenship made a strong breakthrough in the literature at the end of the 1990s (Soysal 1994; Jacobson 1996).

In contrast, we observe an interesting opposite trend whereby local protests, which amounted to nearly one-fifth of all events in the 1975–9 period, went down to less than 1 percent in the last two periods and most importantly following a declining trend from 1980–4 onward. This suggests that a progressive delocalization of protests has occurred since the mid 1970s, at least in the European countries covered by these data. However, this has not gone in favor of the transnational level but has rather strengthened the national character of protest politics. Of course, this tentative conclusion must take into account the fact that we cannot say anything about what happened before or after the years covered by these data, which, however, form a long enough period to say something that is more than anecdotal about the process of scale shift. The important point here is that scale shift, which is usually referred to with respect to a change from a lower to an upper level – most often, from the national to the transnational level – may well reflect an opposite trend – that is, a shift from the transnational to the national level or from the national to the local level.

In sum, concerning the process of scale shift, we can stress three aspects: First, there is no single process of scale shift, but rather a variety of different types of transnationalization of protest politics. Second, while in the long run, protest has certainly shifted its scope from the local to the national level, empirical evidence shows that genuine transnational contention remains quite limited. Third, there is no ineludible move from a lower to an upper level, and sometimes a reverse process can be observed, from the transnational to the national and to the local level.

5 Individualization and Digitalization: The Personalization of Protest Politics

Whether it is myth or reality, it is often claimed that that the earth is becoming more and more globalized. Another such widespread claim is that we live in an increasingly individualized world, one where people are "bowling alone," to use Putnam's (2000) formulation describing the loss of social capital in the American society. No wonder, then, that scholars have pointed to individualization as a further potential process of transformation of protest politics. Once again, this process refers to transformations of political participation more generally, but it has important implications for protest politics more specifically. Here, in fact, we discuss two distinct but interrelated processes: the process of individualization just mentioned, on the one hand, and the process of digitalization, on the other. However, it makes sense to treat these two processes of transformation together, as two sides of the same more general move toward a personalization of contentious politics (Bennet and Segerberg 2013).

Discussions about the personalization of politics have been around for a long time. This term may refer to at least three sorts of phenomena. The first one is something that occurred in party and institutional politics, namely the increasing role of certain political figures and the parallel loss of importance of party structures and more generally organizations in politics (Adam and Maier 2010; Marino 2022; see Garzia et al. 2019 for an annotated bibliography). In short, it refers to the fact that "that individual political actors have become more prominent at the expense of parties and collective identities" (Karvonen 2010: 4). A sizeable share of such discussions have focused on communication styles in personalized politics and therefore on the role of the media therein. As such, it is also linked to the rise of populism in recent years, as the latter is intimately related to how certain politicians communicate and can even be defined as a communicative style (Jagers and Walgrave 2007).

A second kind of personalization of politics is linked to the slogan "the personal is political" (Hanisch 1970), which emerged in the wake of the women's movements of the 1960s and 1970s. This slogan emerged as a criticism of the traditional separation of the private – personal – and public – political – spheres and the related view about gender roles, whereby women were long confined to the former while men were considered more apt for the latter. Instead, feminist activists, but also other movements such as the civil rights and student movements, were affirming the idea that political and personal issues are in many ways intertwined. These movements highlighted, for example, how dynamics of power and authority marginalized certain groups and excluded them from politics. As such, challenging oppression in the private sphere was key for redressing inequalities in the public one.

Here, however, we are not referring to this kind of phenomena, but are rather focusing on yet a third meaning of the term and referring to the personalization of protest politics, hence not focusing so much on formal and institutionalized politics, nor on "the personal is political" in the context of women's issues, but rather on a distinct way in which, increasingly, people – especially young people – engage in more informal and noninstitutional politics today. In this sense, more than "the personal is political," here we are perhaps talking about the extent to which "the political is personal," meaning "how every day political matters might permeate the average person's life" (Ford et al. 2023: 1). While the former slogan stresses that personal issues are also political issues and rests on the idea that political issues cannot be addressed separately from the personal, the latter may be thought of as the fact that politics can also be dealt with in the personal sphere. Let us discuss separately the two processes relating to the personalization of protest politics – individualization and digitalization – and then see how they are connected to each other.

Although individualization arguably denotes something at the same time broader and more profound, discussions of this process in the context of protest politics have often dealt with the rise of a variety of activities that have usually been categorized under such labels as political consumerism (Micheletti 2003; Stolle and Micheletti 2013), everyday politics (Boyte 2004), or lifestyle politics (de Moor 2017).

While it can be traced back much earlier in time, political consumerism became increasingly popular in the aftermath of the antiglobalization protest wave in the late 1990s and early 2000s (Forno and Lorenzini 2022). Traditionally, it refers to boycotting and boycotting – that is, buying or avoiding to buy certain products – or services – for ethical and political reasons. More broadly, political consumerism refers to the purchase of goods and services based, not only on price and product quality, but also on considerations about production methods (i.e., environmental sustainability, workers' rights, human rights) (Forno and Lorenzini 2022: 419).

While keeping its specificities as a distinct mode of participation (Micheletti 2003; Stolle and Micheletti 2013) along with a few others, most notably voting, protesting and, as discussed in this section as well, digital participation (Teocharis and van Deth 2017, 2018; see Giugni and Grasso 2022 for a thorough discussion of each mode), political consumerism has evolved into what has become known as "lifestyle politics." This "refers to the politicization of everyday life choices, including ethically, morally or politically inspired decisions about, for example, consumption, transportation or modes of living" (de Moor 2017: 3). Lifestyle politics has become particularly relevant in advanced capitalist societies since it provides a means for political engagement even within the structural capitalist formation by focusing on small actions and changes that can be applied to improve things. Certainly, it is not the case that one should exist and not the other; indeed, both challenges to structural inequalities and personal behaviors can be effective in different contexts. Yet, while historically labor movements for example focused on broad structural solutions to social problems, lifestyle politics allows also for the expression of identities and beliefs on a smaller scale, which may be particularly suited to capitalist contexts and consumer views of individuals.

As can be seen, in contrast to other modes of political participation, political consumerism and lifestyle politics – especially so the former – give a central place to economic choices. In other words, economic choices take on a political meaning and become ways through which people try to make a difference in their everyday life. In this perspective, scholars have paid attention to so-called alternative forms of resilience (Kousis and Paschou 2017), in particular in the aftermath of the financial crisis of 2008 and the subsequent economic crisis in Europe. These refer to "collective citizen initiatives arising in response to hard economic times, such as solidarity-based exchanges and networks, cooperative structures, barter clubs, credit unions, ethical banks, time banks, alternative social currency, citizens' self-help groups, neighborhood assemblies and social enterprises" (Kousis and Paschou 2017: 136). While signaling "transformations in citizens' practices – from adaptive and alternative to autonomous – aimed towards their future survival" (Kousis and Paschou 2017), these initiatives and activities have a collective nature and therefore, unlike political consumerist and lifestyle politics practices, fall outside of the present discussion about the individualization of protest politics and political participation more generally. These kinds of initiatives and activities are also more closely associated with social movements and protest politics, such as in "sustained community movement organizations" – that is, "social movement organisations that have the peculiarity of mobilising citizens primarily via their purchasing power and for which the main 'battlefield' is represented by the market where SCMOs' members are politically concerned consumers" (Forno and Graziano 2014: 142).

Figure 3 reports a recent effort to illustrate the broad range of strategies, social changes, and forms of action associated with political consumerism and lifestyle politics and that include both individual and collective activities. In this representation, which stresses the transformative and "prefigurative" thrust of these ways of doing politics, different forms of action that may be associated with political consumerism and lifestyle politics may aim at three kinds of transformations, which in turn are related to three different strategies of diffusion: "Transformations associated with lifestyle change seek primarily to 'scale deep' into people's personal life and habits" (Forno and Lorenzini 2022: 423). "The second kind of transformation, fair trade, seeks to 'scale up' to pressure changes in modes of production, aiming at changing how specific firms or sectors produce goods and services" (Forno and Lorenzini 2022: 423). "The third kind of transformation, sustainable communities, is place-based multi-sector coalitions that aim to build alternative, productive, and sustainable networks of production, exchange, and consumption" ... "based on the idea of 'sufficiency,' therefore contrasting not only capitalism expansion of markets but also capitalist accumulation of profit, which is often related to economies of scale (up) to which they oppose the strategy of 'scale out' horizontally through replication" (Forno and Lorenzini 2022: 424).

Research on digital means for protesting and online activism has flourished in the past couple of decades, since internet and social media started to be used for

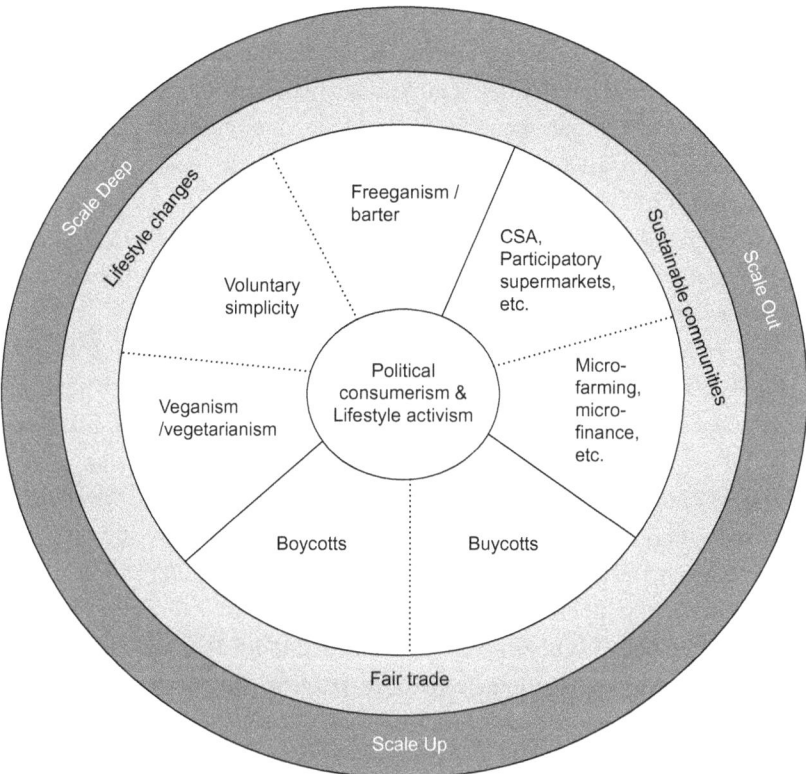

Figure 3 Strategies, social changes, and forms of action associated with political consumerism and lifestyle activism.
Source: Forno and Lorenzini (2022).

those purposes and more generally for political purposes (Earl and Kimport 2011; Gerbaudo 2012; Bennett and Segerberg 2013; Trottier and Fuchs 2015; see Bouliane 2020 for an overview and meta-analysis on the relationship between digital media and engagement in civic and political life). Bennett and Segerberg (2013) have coined the apt expression "logic of connective action" in relation to the rise of a personalized digitally networked politics based on personalized content sharing across media networks, echoing the more traditional "logic of collective action," characterized by high levels of organizational resources and the formation of collective identities. They further noted how communication as an organizational process may replace or supplement more traditional forms of collective action based organizational resource mobilization, leadership, and collective action framing.

Perhaps more than for the other processes of transformation addressed in this Element, the personalization of protest politics opens up a discussion about whether this is something good or bad for social movements, but also more generally in terms of people's political engagement. Concerning the kinds of political activities dealt with in this section, two questions may be seen as epitomizing such a discussion: (1) How political are these activities? (Stolle et al. 2005; Holzer 2006; Graziano and Forno 2012). In other words, are we dealing with forms of contentious politics here? Or does such a personalization of protest politics and more generally of political participation inevitably lead to depoliticization and a shift from public virtue to private life, from public action to private interests (Hirschmann 1982)?

Concerning the first question – to what extent these activities are political – it all depends, of course, on what we mean by "political." The more inclusive the concept is, the more likely that we will find these kinds of individualized activities as political. On the other hand, we do not want to adopt an "everything goes" approach and fall into the trap of what Sartori called "conceptual stretching." Perhaps a balanced midway between these two extremes has been offered by van Deth (2014; see Theocharis and van Deth 2017 for a further elaboration of this approach). This author has proposed a conceptual map distinguishing between minimalist, targeted, and motivational variants of the definition of political participation (plus a fourth variant for nonpolitical activities used for political purposes). Minimalist definitions reflect the traditional view of what political participation is, namely a voluntary behavior done by citizens located in the sphere of government/state/politics. Targeted definitions imply that the activity is located in the sphere of government/state/politics or aimed at solving collective or community problems. Motivational definitions imply that the activity is used to express political aims and intentions of participants – that is, it is politically motivated.

So, following this approach, one can say that individualized or personalized actions such as the ones discussed in this section, even if they might not meet the criteria reflecting more traditional views of political participation or if they do not have an explicit political target, are still political insofar as they are politically motivated. More recently, Theocharis and van Deth (2017) have added definitions according to which an activity might be political because it is performed in a political context, adding what they call circumstantial definitions (in the meantime, motivational definitions also became circumstantial).

Concerning the second aspect – the collective nature of these activities – although protesting can be considered an individual act, most often we think of protest as collective action. As Earl and Kimport (2011: 123) put it, "[i]f you ask almost any social movement scholar what defines protest or a social movement, one of the first elements of their answer will be that people are working together." Surely, deciding not to buy a given product for ethical or political reasons, or to buy one for the same reasons, just like sitting behind the screen of our computer to sign an online petition or post some political content on Instagram are more individualized actions than, say, attending a mass demonstration with thousands of other people or joining a strike. However, precisely because they are political, all such activities have a collective side in some way: They are done knowing – or at least hoping – that others will do the same, and their effectiveness is directly proportional to the number of people carrying them out, at least in the perception of their authors.

The notion of individualized collective action (Micheletti 2003; see also Forno and Lorenzini 2022) aptly captures this intrinsic "collectiveness" of such political actions. Individualized collective action is clearly distinguished from conventional definitions of political participation and is defined as "the practice of responsibility-taking through the creation of everyday settings on the part of citizens alone or together with others to deal with problems which they believe are affecting what they identify as a good life" (Micheletti 2002: 7). In individualized collective action, "large numbers of people join in loosely coordinated activities centered on more personal emotional identifications and rationales . . . and individuals have become fully immersed in consumer cultures and have developed a discerning eye for their political and personal products" (Bennett 2012: 26). Such individualized collective action is often coordinated through digital media technologies (Bennett 2012), which connects the two sides of the process of personalization of protest politics, namely individualization and digitalization. Indeed, participation that is collective on some level may still connect with individuals on an individualized basis and therefore dynamics can be highly complex in terms of whether collective interests or identities can form and under what conditions in these contexts.

Given our focus on protest politics, we should add a third question relating to the implications of the process of individualization and, more generally, personalization: To what extent can these ways of doing politics be considered as forms of protest? The answer to this question obviously depends on how we define protest, what we include and exclude from it. As we said in Section 1, this is not an easy question and there is no definitive answer to it. Moreover, as with any other concept or notion, there is no "right" or "wrong" answer in the end, unless we move too far in terms of the the gap between the concept or notion and the reality the concept or notion is supposed to indicate. To be sure, defining political protest as "a multitude of methods used by individuals and groups within a political system to express their dissatisfaction with the status quo" (Chong 2015: 421) or protest politics as "the deliberate and public use of protest by groups or organizations" (Rucht 2007: 708) does not help much in order to answer the question whether the individual forms of participation as the one described in this section can be considered forms of protest. This simply begs the question of which forms can be considered protest actions.

So one may advance good arguments in favor of both a negative and a positive assessment of the individualization of protest politics. Yet discussions about the positive or negative implications of the personalization of protest politics have perhaps most of the time focused on digitalization.[7] Along these lines, the use of digital forms of protest and, more generally, online political participation is often seen as something problematic. Observers have noted some of the problems relating to this transformation. One such problem is known as "slacktivism." This neologism – sometimes also called, albeit somewhat inaccurately, "clicktivism" or "hashtag activism" – refers, following the Oxford English Dictionary (see also Dennis 2019) to "actions performed via the Internet in support of a political or social cause (e.g. signing an online petition), characterized as requiring little time, effort, or commitment, or as providing more personal satisfaction than public impact." In brief, slacktivism is often seen as making "online activists feel useful and important while having preciously little political impact" (Morozov 2011: 190). Although originally it had a positive connotation (Christensen 2011), the term clearly has come to be seen in a more negative way, meaning something that is done with little effort behind one's computer, tablet, or phone screen and therefore might also be little effective and even harm or undermine "real life" collective action by replacing it. In brief, the negative view about political participation on the internet maintains that online political activities are not less effective in influencing political decisions and that they replace traditional, offline forms of participation (Christensen 2011; Dennis 2019).

Against such negative assessment – often based more on prejudice than on empirical evidence – others have argued that, while the impact of internet campaigns on real-life decisions remains uncertain, they do not seem to replace traditional offline activities (Christensen 2011) but, quite on the contrary, they seem to have a positive impact on online mobilization. Also, social media, such as Facebook and Twitter, may create new opportunities for cognitive engagement, discursive participation, and political mobilization (Dennis 2019).

Others have also stressed the potential positive effects of the digitalization of protest politics, trying to give a more balanced and nuanced judgment. For example, Earl and Kimport (2011) suggest that online activities can facilitate offline protests. They stress more specifically that the Web reduces the costs for

---

[7] Surely digitalization has many other, sometimes quite pernicious, consequences. One of them is relating to the rise of fake news and how this may have triggering effects for protest. Examples may by multiplied in this regard. However, here we focus on those aspects that are more closely related to the personalization of politics.

creating, organizing, and participating in protest activities, on the one hand, and decreases the need for activists to be physically together in order to act together. Similarly, Gaby and Caren (2012) show that social media act as powerful recruiting channels for social movements, helping to rapidly spread and reach broad audiences. Further, Vasi and Suh (2016), on their part, show that social media – in particular Facebook and, to a lesser extent, Twitter – are an important tool for activism and that their use does not necessarily lead to "slacktivism." Instead, social media might help movement mobilization by acting as cyberbrokers coordinating actions between previously unconnected actors. Importantly, however, their research also shows that "organizational resources still matter for the spread of contemporaneous social movements" and their "findings demonstrate that organizational resources matter, even for movements that claim to be decentralized and that rely heavily on cyberbrokerage to connect activists" (Vasi and Suh 2016: 150–151). A variety of other key works have examined these questions from different perspectives (Bennett 2007; Howard 2016; Boulianne 2015; Earl 2022).

Joining these less negative voices, one might add that what some consider as forms of slacktivism might work as what Taylor (1989) has called "abeyance structures." While the latter term was coined with reference to offline organizations and networks, one may expand its meaning to embrace online forms of abeyance which might help a movement keeping alive during hard times and in periods of narrow political opportunities for overt mobilization.

We could go on and on citing authors who see slacktivism – and, more generally, the use of online means of participation – as something positive and others who are more critical, as a large debate has arisen in the past years about these issues, especially in communication studies but also in political sociology. However, this is not the point here. The point is more simple and straightforward: it is undeniable that protest politics – and, more generally, political participation – has become more digital since these means exist, that is, more or less since the mid-2000s. Internet and social media have created new opportunities for organizing, participating, and protesting. On the one hand, this has led to an expansion of the repertoires of contention, as we saw in Section 2. On the other hand, however, the question remains open as to the implications of this change both in terms of the effectiveness of such digital forms of protesting and participating and in terms of the effect of such a digitalization process on more traditional, offline ways of organizing, mobilizing, and protesting.

In a somewhat broader perspective, the increasing personalization of protest politics has sparked discussions about a transformation of citizenship in relation to its participatory dimension and therefore about the existence of different types of citizens in relation to this dimension, especially amongst young people.[8] These different types of citizens are the result of a transformation of the ways in which people – once again, above all, young people – conceive of politics, how they evaluate traditional forms of democracy, and how they think they should act politically, in brief, what they think it is to be a good citizen. Two fundamental changes deserve to be mentioned in this respect. The first change is the one, popularized in particular by Dalton (2009), between a "dutiful citizen," mostly attached to voting as the only legitimate means of political expression in the context of representative democracy, and an "engaged citizen," more focused on direct involvement in protest activities and embracing participatory democracy, starting from about the 1960s.

Related to this shift, some have used the label of "critical citizens" or "dissatisfied democrats" (Dalton 2019; Norris 1999; 2002; 2011) to indicate a group of people who are characterized by a low degree of political trust but a high degree of political efficacy. In other words, critical citizens are highly interested in politics, but show little system support and trust towards established political actors and institutions, are cynical about established politics, and at the same time confident that both individual and collective action can help change things. People with this profile reflect well the shift to political consumerism and lifestyle politics (Forno and Lorenzini 2022), but it has also been shown to be particularly active in social movements and more specifically in street demonstrations (Giugni and Grasso 2019).

More recently – say, from the 2000s onward – the figure of the self-actualized citizen (Bennett 2008) has emerged, as said, particularly within the youngest generations, also in relation to the processes of individualization and digitalization. Self-actualized citizens emphasize quality of personal life and social relations, especially in relation to the rise of the digital age and its impact on citizenship for young people (Bennett 2008). As a result, while not necessarily abandoning engagement in protest activities or more institutional forms of participation such as voting for that matter, they express political choices through actions in their everyday life, as part of lifestyle politics.

To be sure, while we have stressed changes over time, this is not to say that one type of citizen has necessarily replaced an older type – specifically, that the self-actualized citizen has replaced the engaged or critical citizen which in turn had replaced the dutiful citizen. A more plausible and realistic representation consists in saying that all these profiles coexist in today's political landscape, although dutiful citizens are most likely less numerous today than they were, say, fifty years

---

[8] Citizenship may be thought as having three main dimensions, all related to the underlying condition of civic equality: membership or belonging, rights, and participation (Bellamy 2008). Here we are referring to the latter dimension.

ago, and the same might occur with self-actualized citizens as compared to engaged citizens in a few years from now. In other words, to sum up and perhaps oversimplify a more articulated discussion ad above all a more complex reality, we may see four types of citizens in the political landscape today, resulting from the transformations we have been discussing: a declining group of dutiful citizens attached to representative democracy and institutional participation, mainly voting; a now well-established group of engaged citizens embracing participatory democracy and more directly involved in politics through protest or other non-institutional means; a specific group of critical citizens, attached to democracy but not to representative democracy – dissatisfied democrats, in that sense – and characterized by low levels of political trust but high levels of political efficacy; and – most often young – actualized or self-actualized citizens who prefer to engage in more individualized forms in their everyday life and make their lifestyle a way to do politics, including by using digital means of political expression.

Once again, just as we did for the other transformations discussed in previous sections, we can ask ourselves to what extent the personalization of protest politics has actually taken place. To do this, we may ask more specifically whether, on the one hand, individualized and, on the other hand, digital forms of protest have replaced more traditional, offline forms, or at least are on the rise. Protest event or claims-making data are of little help here as, almost by definition, more personalized forms of protest largely escape media coverage. To get a grasp on them, we need to resort to survey data.

Scholars noted that political consumerist activities have increased since the early 2000s, especially after the anti-globalization protest wave (Forno and Lorenzini 2022). Our own analysis of EVS data, however, shows a slightly different picture. If we look back at Table 2, we can see that the share of people who said they have ever joined a boycott has remained quite stable between the early 1980s and the late 2010s, and the same holds for those declaring that they might do it. The same indicator using the ESS data provides a bit more evidence of growth, as the share of people who said they have boycotted certain products for ethical or political reasons in the last 12 months has risen overall from 16.5 percent in 2002 to 22.3 percent in 2020. Here the different ways in which the question was asked – "ever done" in the EVS, "last 12 months" in the ESS – might in part explain this difference.

Is this stable development over time in the adoption of political consumerist practices due to the fact that we looked at the whole population while this is something that concerns above all youth? In fact, if we look at respondents younger than 35 or even younger than 25, the picture does not really change much. In fact, for these two groups, boycotting has even declined during the period covered by the EVS data, while the trend is quite similar to that of the general population in the ESS data.[9] So, even if we focus on the age cohorts which are supposed to be particularly involved in this kind of practices, we do not really see strong evidence of an increase.

We must say, however, that political consumerism is only one side of lifestyle politics – and, more broadly, of a shift towards more individualized political activities. So, to get a more accurate and comprehensive picture we should also look at other ethically or politically motivated choices people – especially youngsters – make in their everyday life, such as for example adhering to "soft mobility" or adopting measures to reduce the usage of fossil energy sources. Unfortunately it is still hard to find longitudinal survey data that includes such measures. For sure, there are aggregate data on this, but which cannot be associated to an individual ethical or political choice and therefore can hardly be used as indicators of lifestyle politics.

Conducting the same exercise and looking for empirical evidence of an increase in online political activities entails the risk of introducing a bias if we look at the same 40-year period of time, as the channels and means to do this kind of activities simply did not exist, say, 20 or 25 years ago. What we could do is to see whether we observe a more recent upward trend. Unfortunately, measures of online political activities in the available general population surveys as the ones we used so far are scarce. The EVS/WVS include a few measures in the last wave, but due to the staggered data collection they cannot be used for our purpose of assessing changes over time. The ESS has one indicator – posted or shared anything about politics online last 12 months – that could be used, but only for the last waves. The data show that, overall, the share of people doing this kind of online political activity is rather stable (16.4 percent in 2016, 15.5 percent in 2018, and 16.4 percent in 2020). Such a stability applies also if we focus on respondents younger than 35 or younger than 25 – since these are typically activities often done by young people as compared to the general population – although the numbers go up for these younger cohorts.

For a somewhat longer outlook we can use the Eurostat data, which include some aggregate-level measures of the political use of the internet. Table 5 shows the evolution in time of four indicators: taking part in online consultations or

---

[9] According to the EVS data, share of respondents younger than 35 who said they have already joined in boycotts went from 11.9 percent to 9.8 percent, while the share of respondents younger than 25 who said they have already joined in boycotts went from 10.1 percent to 9.0 percent. According to the ESS data, the share of respondents younger than 35 who said they have boycotted certain products in the last 12 months went from 16.7 percent in 2002 to 23.7 percent in 2020, while the share of respondents younger than 25 who said they have boycotted certain products in the last 12 months went from 14.3 percent in 2002 to 21.5 percent in 2020.

Table 5 Use of internet for political purposes in the European Union (twenty-seven countries) from 2008 to 2023 (percentages)

	2011	2013	2015	2017	2019	2021	2022	2023
Taking part in online consultations or voting to define civic or political issues (e.g. urban planning, signing a petition)	7.4	7.6	7.4	8.0	9.5	8.5	8.4	8.5
Expressing opinions on civic or political issues on websites or in social media (e.g. Facebook, Twitter, Instragram, YouTube)	-	-	-	-	-	14.1	14.3	14.9
Posting opinions on civic or political issues via websites (e.g. blogs, social networks, etc.)	-	11.0	10.0	10.8	10.6	-	-	-
Civic or political participation	-	14.3	13.5	14.5	15.6	17.4	17.6	18.3

Source: Eurostat (https://ec.europa.eu/eurostat).

voting to define civic or political issues (such as urban planning or signing a petition), expressing opinions on civic or political issues on websites or in social media (such as Facebook, Twitter, Instragram, or YouTube), posting opinions on civic or political issues via websites (such as blogs or social networks), and a more general measure of online civic or political participation.

The data are a bit scattered and partial, but they allow to draw some conclusions in relation to people's online political activities. The first thing we can say when looking at these numbers is that the share of people engaging online varies depending on the type of activity, just as they vary across countries as well, although here we focus on overall trends. In particular, we see that a substantial number of people are involved civic or political participation on the internet. The figures for the more recent years are not that far from those reported for example by Theocharis and van Deth (2017) in their analysis of digitally networked participation (they report 22 percent). While the indicators used are not exactly the same, this provides some reliability to these data. Most importantly for our present purpose, the share of people involved in such online activities displays an upward trend, although the rise is far from dramatic. The other three indicators, however, are all more stable over time and do not show any trend whatsoever.

What can we conclude from all these numbers? Generally speaking, beyond differences across countries and contexts which we have not dealt with here, online activities have become widespread among the general population over the past few years. This is all the more true for the youngest generations. However, while we do observe an upward trend in certain online activities, such an increase is not as strong as one may expect. So while internet and social media have created new opportunities for political engagement, including in ways which we may assimilate to protest activities, the breakthrough of online political activism seems to have occurred right after these opportunities emerged – that is, roughly since the mid 2000s. Furthermore, it is likely that, among the possible ways in which one can use the internet for political purposes, those activities that require less effort and commitment – often depicted as "slacktivism" – are the most popular, whereas more demanding activities – including those relating to protest politics – such as organizing political initiatives are less widespread, just like what happens for similar activities offline.

In sum, concerning the processes of individualization and digitalization – which we have discussed together in relation to the personalization of protest politics – we can stress several key aspects: first, that the personalization and digitalization of politics have gone hand in hand; second, that these processes challenge the centrality of collectiveness that has traditionally been critical for making sense of protest and political participation more generally, even if indirectly; third, this process has meant that new forms of political engagement have proliferated that tend to be much more individualized than the attendance of a protest or engagement that underpins participation in a protest movement.

6 Conclusion

In this Element we have tried to do three things. First, we discussed four key processes of transformation of protest politics addressed in the social movement and political participation literatures. Second, when available, we examined empirical evidence of these processes of transformation, mainly with illustrative purposes. Third, we adopted a "healthy skepticism" (Pettigrew 1996), subjecting the four processes of transformation to critical scrutiny, also based on that evidence.

We can summarize our discussion as follows. Protest politics has transformed over the years: It has expanded in its forms and modes, it has become more "normal" – both in terms of the frequency and legitimacy of certain forms such as the mass demonstration and in terms of the variety of people who become have come to be involved in protest activities – it has shifted in its scale to some extent, and it is increasingly individualized and digitalized. This may be understood in broad terms as a continuous process of expansion, normalization, scale shift, and personalization. However, we can identify certain historical phases during which one or more of these processes of transformation have been boosted. In this view, we may identify four major historical phases: a first phase marking the shift from the old to the new repertoire of contention at the turn of the eighteenth and nineteenth centuries, as masterfully described by Tilly (1986, 1995) and that not only brought about an expansion of action repertoires but also a shift from the local to the national level; a second phase around the late 1960s and early 1970s marked by the rise of the new social movements, which contributed to further expanding the forms and content of protest politics and also to a further normalization of certain forms of action; a third phase at the turn of the millennium, when global justice movements helped shift the scale of contention from the national to the transnational level; and a fourth phase from the mid 2000s characterized by an increasing individualization and digitalization of protest, two sides of what we have called the personalization of protest politics.

At the same time, however, we should be careful not to be overenthusiastic about these transformations: new forms of protest remain limited within known and culturally determined repertoires (and old forms are sometimes abandoned because no longer effective, legitimate, or acceptable); protest (including demonstrations) remains something that people use relatively episodically, though in a "modular" way (McPhail 1993; Tarrow 1993, 2011 [1994]), meaning that it can be used by different people for different purposes and in different contexts; little change of scale has taken place (with the national level remaining predominant); and individualization and digitalization concerns mostly if not exclusively certain social categories so far (most notably the younger generations).

Do the four processes of transformation exhaust the range of possible processes of change of protest politics we may think of? Certainly not. About three decades ago, Kriesi (1996) suggested that social movement organizations (SMOs) may undergo a transformation of their goal orientations and action repertoires along three directions: commercialization (when the SMO loses both the direct participation of its constituency and the orientation of its activities toward the authorities' orientation in favor of a constituency/client orientation), involution (when the SMO keeps the direct participation of its constituency but loses the authorities' orientation in favor of a constituency/client orientation), institutionalization (when the SMO keeps the authorities' orientation but loses the direct participation of its constituency), or radicalization (a transformation whereby the SMO keeps these two original features, perhaps even strengthening them, but becomes more radical in its goals and/or its actions).

Some of these changes could also to some extent be related to further potential processes of transformation of protest politics more generally. Take the two processes most often referred to in the literature: institutionalization and radicalization. Concerning the former aspect, one may be tempted, inspired by the thinking of Weber and Michels, to say that there is a sort of "iron law of oligarchy" that applies to the social movement sector and to protest politics more generally. This would imply that movements start off as very informal, grassroots, and perhaps even spontaneous actors and activities to then transform into something more structured through a process of institutionalization by which we mean, among other things, an increasing formalization, professionalization, and bureaucratization of the initial collective actor. While this is indeed true in many cases – think, for example, to the original green parties in the environmental movements of the 1960s and 1970s – at least two objections may be raised against such an argument: first, that it would apply to social movement organizations rather than to movements as such; second, that it would apply to some organizations but not to others. As a result, it is hard to think of a general trend going from informal, perhaps even spontaneous movements and protest to more institutionalized, formalized, and institutionalized collective actors that would lose their movement-like characteristics.

Such an inescapable fate is even less plausible when it comes to radicalization. The latter is in some way the opposite of institutionalization. Radicalization may refer to either means or ends, or both. In other words, an actor, organization, or movement may on the one hand become more radical in its claims – meaning going to the root of things rather than remaining on the surface – but on the other hand, it may also use less peaceful tactics and become more confrontational, including sometimes the use of violence or other constraints. Research on protest politics and social movements has overwhelmingly focused on the latter aspect (but see, e.g., Gamson 1990 for a work paying attention also to the other aspect). Without going into the details of quite a large literature, we believe it is fair to say that scholarship, rather than pointing to the existence of a trend toward more or, conversely, less radical protests, shows how radicalization is a dynamic phenomenon that is contingent upon the interaction between certain endogenous characteristics of movements and the external environment – especially in terms of the state and police exerting repression – hence displaying significant variations both across space and over time (della Porta 2018).

Both institutionalization and radicalization are far from ineluctable universal processes. Quite the contrary, they are very much context-dependent. As political opportunity theorists have repeatedly shown, social movements are strongly dependent on their broader institutional context (see Kriesi 2004 and McAdam and Tarrow 2019 for overviews). Paths toward institutionalization or, conversely, radicalization result from the interplay between the structure of political opportunities – meaning both in their institutional and discursive sides – and the endogenous characteristics of movements (Kriesi et al. 1995; McAdam 1999). Loosely structured grassroots movements and protests continue to emerge; some transform into something more "institutional" – sometimes an interest group, sometimes even a party – but most of them do not. As institutional channeling theory argues, such a process may occur insofar as the broader environment of movements and protest is conducive to it (Jenkins and Eckert 1986; McCarthy et al 1991; Jenkins 1998). Similarly, radicalization owes much to the interactions between movements and protesters, on the one hand, and the state – including police behavior – on the other (Ellefsen 2021).

Another potential process of transformation resides in a "judicialization" of protest politics, meaning an increasingly important role of legal mobilization (Taylor and Tarrow 2024). In this context, protest becomes increasingly practiced through judicial means where political challenges become fought through laws or the courts rather than in the public sphere of debate and contestation of ideas. For example, environmental campaigns are increasingly contested in the judicial sphere, and other social movement battles such as for LGBTQ+ or women's rights come to be contested through legal means, and this phenomenon is particularly developed in the United States. However, increasingly, there have been instances also in Europe. The judicialization of protest may be related to broader processes of depoliticization in the public sphere where the absence of suitable collective action mechanisms means that other means are often preferable for canvassing for change.

This leads us to conclude with a few words about the future and specifically about where protest politics is heading. This follows naturally from the four processes of transformation we have been discussing throughout this Element. To begin with, protest politics might carry on its secular process of expansion started at the turn of the eighteenth and nineteenth centuries and continued with the continuous "invention" of new forms of protest. These may include those forms exploiting the technological advances made in the past few decades. This is quite plausible, although one should also stress that the modalities through which ordinary people have at their disposal to make their claims heard are not infinite. Quite on the contrary, as Tilly (1986, 1995) has shown, the repertoires of contention characterizing specific epochs are quite limited in the end.

Perhaps less likely is that protest will further normalize. As we have tried to show, the process of normalization of protest seems to have slowed down its pace in the past few decades. Furthermore, this process concerns only certain forms of protest – most notably, mass demonstrations – while other, more radical forms have not really normalized, for that matter. However, one cannot totally exclude that mass demonstrations will become even more legitimate and frequent, nor that other forms will undergo a similar process in the future.

In addition to the process of normalization of protest, we have also been discussing, with a less skeptical stance, the normalization of the protesters. Here we could hypothesize that the participation of people in protest activities, especially those that are not too costly or risky, will continue, leading to an increasing resemblance between those who protest and those who do not. Yet, once again, we have reasons to believe that at some point such a closing of the gap will stop or at least reach its limits. A similar reasoning applies to the idea, mentioned in relation to the normalization of the protesters in Section 3, that movements addressing "old" – economic and redistributive – issues and movements that address "new" – social justice and emancipatory – issues have gotten closer to each other in terms of sociodemographic background and value orientations of their constituencies. Will this gap narrow further in the future? Or even: Will such blurring of the boundaries start cutting across the left–right ideological divide, as the French "yellow vest" movements – whose social composition included both people from the left and from the right of the political or ideological spectrum – seem to suggest? Or will polarization take over and put a stop to this process? Once again, it is hard to make a strong argument in favor of one or the other scenario, but if we were to bet on either one, a scenario in which distinctions between movements, and above all between ideological divides, will remain in the future is arguably more plausible.

What about scale shift? As we have seen, a long-term process has taken place in which protest, once confined to local settings, has then scaled up first to the national level and then – accelerated by the process of globalization – to the supranational or transnational level. Will this process continue, particularly for what concerns the shift beyond the national level? The answer to this question depends on an assessment of how far the process of denationalization will go and the extent to which opportunities for mobilization beyond the national state will emerge in the future. On both counts, prospects rather suggest that scale shift has perhaps reached its limits, at least in this historical phase. For one thing, the shift from the local to the national level has long occurred and it is hard to think of a further increase in this respect. For the other, the loss of power and centrality of the national state, proclaimed by some, has not occurred, or at best to a limited extent for what concerns politics. For sure, local and national protests are not ready to disappear. Quite on the contrary, they seem to even have increased. Most protests today still raise local or national issues. Moreover, they generally involve local or national actors and coalitions. Finally, they tend to be addressed at local or national targets.

Finally, protest politics might become more "personalized," either in terms of a more frequent use of online forms of protesting, of an increasingly "individualized" approach to political participation, or both. This trend toward a personalization of protest politics and more generally political participation can hardly be questioned. Forms of activism consisting in politically motivated choice made in one own's everyday life have become increasingly popular, especially amongst the younger generations. Furthermore, online means of carrying out protest activities and doing politics have entered the repertoire of participation in the past few years. This trend will probably continue in the near future, and perhaps also in the more distant future. The main point is not whether such more recent forms of protest are important and will play an even more important role in the future. Probably yes. The main point is rather whether they will supersede the more "traditional" – or normal – forms, made above all of offline collective actions, as embodied in the archetypical form of protest today, namely the mass demonstration, but also other, more confrontational and radical activities. In this regard, as we have seen, we have little evidence that such personalized and digitalized forms of activism will replace more traditional forms. The most plausible, albeit admittedly little, engaging prediction or forecast we can offer is that protest politics, even more than in the past, will be characterized by a blend of older, more traditional features and some innovation brought about by changing social habits or new technologies.

The share of the ones and the others might change across contexts as well as over time and also across social sectors and generations, but ordinary people will arguably continue mounting organized collective efforts addressed to the targets they consider most relevant for their claims and most likely to respond to them positively.

References

Acik, N. (2013). Reducing the Participation Gap in Civic Engagement: Political Consumerism in Europe. *European Sociological Review*, 29(6), 1309–22.

Adam, S. & Maier, M. (2010). Personalization of Politics: A Critical Review and Agenda for Research. *Annals of the International Communication Association*, 34(1), 213–57.

Almeida, P. & Chase-Dunn, C. (2018). Globalization and Social Movements. *Annual Review of Sociology*, 44, 189–211.

Balme, R. & Chabanet, D. (2002). Action collective et gouvernance de l'Union européenne. In R. Balme, D. Chabanet & V. Wright, eds., *L'action collective en Europe: Collective Action in Europe*. Paris: Presses de Sciences Po, pp. 21–120.

Balme, R. & Chabanet, D. (2008). *European Governance and Democracy: Power and Protest in the EU*. Lanham, MD: Rowman and Littlefield.

Barnes, S. H. & Kaase, M., eds. (1979). *Political Action: Mass Participation in Five Western Democracies*. Beverly Hills, CA: Sage.

Beerten, R., Billiet, J., Carton, A. & Swyngedouw, M. (1997). *1995 General Election Study Belgium: Codebook and Questionnaire*. Leuven: Interuniversitair Steunpunt Politieke-Opinieonderzoek.

Bell, D. (1960). *The End of Ideology: On the Exhaustion of Political Ideas in the Fifties*. Glencoe, IL: The Free Press.

Bellamy, R. (2008). *Citizenship: A Very Short Introduction*. Oxford: Oxford University Press.

Bennett, L., ed. (2007). *Civic Life Online: Learning How Digital Media Can Engage Youth*. Cambridge, MA: MIT Press.

Bennett, L. (2008). Changing Citizenship in the Digital Age. In L. Bennett, ed., *Civic Life Online: Learning How Digital Media Can Engage Youth*. Cambridge, MA: MIT Press, pp. 1–24.

Bennett, L. (2012). The Personalization of Politics: Political Identity, Social Media, and Changing Patterns of Participation. *Annals of the American Academy of Political and Social Science*, 644, 20–39.

Bennett, W. L. & Segerberg, A. (2013). *The Logic of Connective Action: Digital Media and the Personalization of Contentious Politics*. Cambridge: Cambridge University Press.

Bordogna, L. (2010). Strikes in Europe: Still a Decade of Decline or the Eve of a New Upsurge? *Indian Journal of Industrial Relations*, 45(4), 658–70.

Boulianne, S. (2015). Social Media Use and Participation: A Meta-analysis of Current Research. *Information, Communication & Society*, 18(5), 524–38.

Boulianne, S. (2020). Twenty Years of Digital Media Effects on Civic and Political Participation. *Communication Research*, 47(7), 947–66.

Boyte, C. H. (2004). *Everyday Politics: Reconnecting Citizens and Public Life*. Philadelphia: University of Pennsylvania Press.

Buechler, S. M. (2004). The Strange Career of Strain and Breakdown Theories of Collective Action. In D. A. Snow, S. A. Soule & H. Kriesi, eds., *The Blackwell Companion to Social Movements*. Oxford: Blackwell, pp. 47–66.

Castelli Gattinara P., Froio C. & Pirro A. (2022). Far-Right Protest Mobilisation in Europe: Grievances, Opportunities and Resources. *European Journal of Political Research*, 61(4), 1019–41.

Chase-Dunn, C. & Almeida, P. (2020). *Global Struggles and Social Change: From Prehistory to World Revolution in the Twenty-First Century*. Baltimore, MD: Johns Hopkins University Press.

Chong, D. (2015 [2001]). Political Protest and Civil Disobedience. In J. D. Wright, ed., *International Encyclopedia of the Social & Behavioral Sciences*, 2nd ed. Amsterdam: Elsevier, pp. 421–6.

Christensen, H. S. (2011). Political Activities on the Internet: Slacktivism or Political Participation by Other Means? *First Monday*, 16(2). https://doi.org/10.5210/fm.v16i2.3336.

Cinalli, M. & Giugni, M. (2013). Guest Editorial: Public Discourses about Muslims and Islam in Europe. *Ethnicities*, 13(2), 131–46.

Cinalli, M. & Giugni, M. (2016). Introduction to the Special Issue: Citizens' Responses to the European Economic Crisis in the Public Domain. *Politics and Policy*, 44(3), 388–99.

Coffé, H. & Bolzendahl, C. (2010). Same Game, Different Rules? Gender Differences in Political Participation. *Sex Roles*, 62(5), 318–33.

Dalton, R. J. (2004). *Democratic Challenges, Democratic Choices: The Erosion of Political Support in Advanced Industrial Democracies*. Oxford: Oxford University Press.

Dalton, R. J. (2008 [1988]). *Citizen Politics: Public Opinion and Political Parties in Advanced Industrial Democracies*, 5th ed. Washington, DC: CQ Press.

Dalton, R. J. (2009). *The Good Citizen: How a Younger Generation Is Reshaping American Politics*. Washington, DC: CQ Press.

Dalton, R. J. (2019 [1988]). *Citizen Politics: Public Opinion and Political Parties in Advanced Industrial Democracies*, 7th ed. New York: Chatham House.

della Porta, D. (1996). Social Movements and the State: Thoughts on the Policing of Protest. In D. McAdam, J. D. McCarthy & M. N. Zald, eds., *Comparative Perspectives on Social Movements: Political Opportunities, Mobilizing Structures, and Cultural Framings*. Cambridge: Cambridge University Press, pp. 62–92.

della Porta, D. (2015). *Social Movements in Times of Austerity: Bringing Capitalism Back into Protest Analysis*. Cambridge: Polity.

della Porta, D. (2018). Radicalization: A Relational Perspective. *Annual Review of Political Science*, 21, 461–74.

della Porta, D., Andretta, M., Mosca, L. & Reiter, H. (2006). *Globalization from Below: Transnational Activists and Protest Networks*. Minneapolis: University of Minnesota Press.

della Porta, D. & Caiani, M. (2011). *Social Movements and Europeanization*. Oxford: Oxford University Press.

della Porta, D., Kriesi, H. & Rucht, D., eds. (1999). *Social Movements in a Globalizing World*. London: Macmillan.

della Porta, D. & Tarrow, S., eds. (2005). *Transnational Protest and Global Activism*. Lanham, MD: Rowman and Littlefield.

de Moor, J. (2017). Lifestyle Politics and the Concept of Political Participation. *Acta Politica*, 52(2), 179–97.

Dennis, J. (2019). *Beyond Slacktivism: Political Participation on Social Media*. Cham: Palgrave Macmillan.

Diani, M. (2015). *The Cement of Civil Society: Studying Networks in Localities*. Cambridge: Cambridge University Press.

Dolezal, M. & Hutter, S. (2012, November 9–10). The Europeanization of Protest Politics: A Comparative Study of EU and Non-EU Member States. Paper prepared for presentation at the 2nd Research Conference of the ÖFG Working Group on Democracy, "Civil Society and Democracy." Vienna, Austria.

Earl, J. & Kimport, K. (2011). *Digitally Enabled Social Change: Activism in the Internet Age*. Cambridge, MA: MIT Press.

Eggert, N. & Giugni, M. (2012). Homogenizing "Old" and "New" Social Movements: A Comparison of Participants in May Day and Climate Change Demonstrations. *Mobilization*, 17(3), 335–48.

Eggert, N. & Giugni, M. (2015). Does the Class Cleavage Still Matter? The Social Composition of Participants in Demonstrations Addressing Redistributive and Cultural Issues in Three Countries. *International Sociology*, 30(1), 21–38.

Ellefsen, R. (2021). The Unintended Consequences of Escalated Repression. *Mobilization*, 26(1), 87–108.

Favre, P., Fillieule, O. & Mayer, N. (1997). La fin d'une étrange lacune de la sociologie des mobilisations. L'étude par sondage des manifestants: fondements théoriques et solutions techniques. *Revue Française de Science Politique*, 47(1), 3–28.

Ford, B. Q., Feinberg, M., Lassetter, B., Thai, S. & Gatchpazian, A. (2023). The Political Is Personal: The Costs of Daily Politics. *Journal of Personality and Social Psychology: Attitudes and Social Cognition*. https://doi.org/10.1037/pspa0000335.

Forno, F. & Graziano, P. (2014). Sustainable Community Movement Organisations. *Journal of Consumer Culture*, 14(2), 139–57.

Forno, F. & Lorenzini, J. (2022). Political Consumerism and Lifestyle Activism. In M. Giugni & M. Grasso, eds., *The Oxford Handbook of Political Participation*. Oxford: Oxford Unversity Press, pp. 417–34.

Franzosi, R. (2023). Strikes. In M. Grasso & M. Giugni, eds., *Elgar Encyclopedia of Political Sociology*. Cheltenham: Edward Elgar, pp. 576–8.

Fuchs, D. (1991). The Normalization of the Unconventional: New Forms of Political Action and New Social Movements. In G. Meyer & F. Ryszka, eds., *Political Participation and Democracy in Poland and West Germany*. Warsaw: Wydaeca, pp. 148–69.

Fureix, E. (2015). Le charivari politique: Un rite de surveillance civique dans les années 1830. In A. Beaurepaire-Hernandez & J. Guedj, eds., *L'entre-deux electoral: Une autre histoire de la représentation politique en France (XIXe–XXe siècle)*. Rennes: Presses Universitaires de Rennes, pp. 53–70.

Gaby, S. & Caren, N. (2012). Occupy Online: How Cute Old Men and Malcolm X Recruited 400,000 US Users to OWS on Facebook. *Social Movement Studies* 11(3–4), 367–74.

Gamson, W. A. (1990). *The Strategy of Social Protest*. 2nd ed. Belmont, CA: Wadsworth.

Gamson, W. A. (1992). *Talking Politics*. Cambridge: Cambridge University Press.

Garzia, D. & Ferreira da Silva, F. (2019). Personalization of Politics. *Oxford Bibliographies in Political Science*. https://doi.org/10.1093/obo/9780199756223-0263.

Gerbaudo, P. (2012). *Tweets and the Streets: Social Media and Contemporary Activism*. London: Pluto Press.

Giugni, M., ed. (2010). *The Contentious Politics of Unemployment in Europe: Welfare States and Political Opportunities*. Houndmills: Palgrave.

Giugni, M., Bandler, M. & Eggert, N. (2006). The Global Justice Movement: How Far Does the Classic Social Movement Agenda Go in Explaining Transnational Contention? Programme Paper Number 24, UNRISD, Geneva.

Giugni, M. & Grasso, M. (2019). *Street Citizens: Protest Politics and Social Movement Activism in the Age of Globalization*. Cambridge: Cambridge University Press.

Giugni, M. & Grasso, M. (2020). Nothing Is Lost, Nothing Is Created, Everything Is Transformed: From Labor Movements to Anti-austerity Protests, in C. Flesher Fominaya & R. A. Feenstra, eds., *Routledge Handbook of Contemporary European Movements: Protest in Turbulent Times*. London: Routledge, pp. 129–41.

Giugni, M. and M. T. Grasso (2021) Living with Hard Times: Europeans in the Great Recession. Colchester: European Consortium for Political Research (ECPR) Press.

Giugni, M. & Grasso, M. (2022). Protest Participation. In M. Giugni & M. Grasso, eds., *The Oxford Handbook of Political Participation*. Oxford: Oxford Unversity Press, pp. 396–416.

Grasso, M. T. & Giugni, M. (2015). Are Anti-austerity Movements "Old" or "New"? In M. Giugni & M. T. Grasso, eds., *Austerity and Protest: Popular Contention in Times of Economic Crisis*. London: Routledge, pp. 57–82.

Grasso, M. T. & Giugni, M. (2016). Do Issues Matter? Anti-austerity Protests' Composition, Value Orientations, and Action Repertoires Compared. In T. Davies, H. Ryan & A. Peña, eds., *Research in Social Movements, Conflicts and Change*. Greenwich, CT: JAI Press, pp. 31–58.

Grasso, M. and M. Giugni (2024) "Gendered opportunities across modes of political participation: A macro-micro analysis of the gender gap" European Journal of Politics and Gender https://doi.org/10.1332/251510 88Y2024D000000055.

Grasso, M. T. & Smith, K. (2022). Gender Inequalities in Political Participation and Political Engagement among Young People in Europe: Are Young Women Less Politically Engaged than Young Men? *Politics*, 42(1), 39–57.

Graziano, P. & Forno, F. (2012). Political Consumerism and New Forms of Political Participation: The "Gruppi Di Acquisto Solidale" in Italy. *Annals of the American Academy of Political and Social Science*, 644, 121–33.

Goldstone, J. A. (1998). Social Movements or Revolutions? On the Evolution and Outcomes of Collective Action. In M. Giugni, D. McAdam & C. Tilly, eds., *From Contention to Democracy*. Lanham, MD: Rowman and Littlefield, pp. 125–47.

Hanisch, C. (1970). The Personal Is Political. In S. Firestone and A. Koedt, eds., *Notes from the Second Year: Women's Liberation*. New York: Radical Feminism, pp. 113–16.

Hirschmann, A. O. (1982). *Shifting Involvements: Private Interest and Public Action*. Princeton, NJ: Princeton University Press.

Holecz, V. (2023). Young Citizens: A Study on Shaping Conceptions, Overcoming Obstacles, and Political Participation in Times of Increasing Inequalities. PhD Thesis. University of Geneva.

Holzer, B. (2006). Political Consumerism between Individual Choice and Collective Action: Social Movements, Role Mobilization and Signalling. *International Journal of Consumer Studies*, 30, 405–415.

Howard, P. N., Savage, S., Flores-Saviaga, C., Toxtli, C., & Monroy-Hernández, A. (2016). Social Media, Civic Engagement, and the Slacktivism Hypothesis: Lessons from Mexico's "El Bronco." *Journal of International Affairs*, 70(1), 55–73.

Hutter, S. (2014a). Protest Event Analysis and Its Offspring. In D. della Porta, ed., *Methodological Practices in Social Movement Research*. Oxford: Oxford University Press, pp. 335–67.

Hutter, S. (2014b). *Protesting Culture and Economics in Western Europe: New Cleavages in Left and Right Politics*. Minneapolis: University of Minnesota Press.

Imig, D. (2002). Contestation in the Streets: European Protest and the Emerging Euro-Polity. *Comparative Political Studies*, 35(8), 914–33.

Imig, D. & Tarrow, S. (2001). Studying Contention in an Emerging Polity. In D. Imig & S. Tarrow, eds., *Contentious Europeans: Protest and Politics in an Emerging Polity*. Lanham, MD: Rowman and Littlefield, pp. 3–26.

Inglehart, R. (1977). *The Silent Revolution: Changing Values and Political Styles among Western Publics*. Princeton, NJ: Princeton University Press.

Jacobson, D. (1996). *Rights across Borders: Immigration and the Decline of Citizenship*. Baltimore, MD: Johns Hopkins University Press.

Jagers, J. & Walgrave, S. (2007). Populism as Political Communication Style: An Empirical Study of Political Parties' Discourse in Belgium. *European Journal of Political Research*, 46(3), 319–45.

Jenkins, J. C. (1998). Channeling Social Protest: Foundation Patronage of Contemporary Social Movements. In W. W. Powell & E. S. Clemens, eds, *Private Action and the Public Good*. New Haven, CT: Yale University Press, pp. 206–17.

Jenkins, J. C. & Eckert, C. M. (1986). Channeling Black Insurgency: Elite Patronage and Professional Social Movement Organisations in the Development of the Black Movement. *American Sociological Review*, 51(6), 812–29.

Kaldor, M. (2003). *Global Civil Society: An Answer to War*. Cambridge: Polity.

Karvonen, L. (2010). *The Personalisation of Politics: A Study of Parliamentary Democracies*. Colchester: ECPR Press.

Keck, M. E. & Sikkink, K. (1998). *Activists beyond Borders: Advocacy Networks in International Politics*. Ithaca, NY: Cornell University Press.

Klandermans, B., van Stekelenburg, J. & Walgrave, S. (2014). Comparing Street Demonstrations. *International Sociology*, 29(6): 493–503.

Koopmans, R. (1993). The Dynamics of Protest Waves: West Germany, 1965 to 1989. *American Sociological Review*, 58(5), 637–58.

Koopmans, R. & Rucht, D. (2002). Protest Event Analysis. In B. Klandermans & S. Staggenborg, eds., *Methods of Social Movement Research*. Minneapolis: University of Minnesota Press, pp. 231–59.

Koopmans, R. & Statham, P. (1999). Political Claims Analysis: Integrating Protest Event and Political Discourse Approaches. *Mobilization*, 4(2), 203–21.

Koopmans, R., Statham, P., Giugni, M. & Passy, F. (2005). *Contested Citizenship: Immigration and Cultural Diversity in Europe*. Minneapolis: University of Minnesota Press.

Kousis, M. & Giugni, M. (2020). Guest Editorial: Claiming and Framing Youth in the Public Domain during Times of Increasing Inequalities. *American Behavioral Scientist*, 64(5), 567–73.

Kousis, M. & Paschou, M. (2017). Alternative Forms of Resilience: A Typology of Approaches for the Study of Citizen Collective Responses in Hard Economic Times. *Partecipazione e Conflitto*, 10(1), 136–68.

Kriesi, H. (1989). New Social Movements and the New Class in the Netherlands. *American Journal of Sociology*, 94(5), 1078–1117.

Kriesi, H. (1996). The Organizational Structure of New Social Movements in a Political Context. In D. McAdam, J. D. McCarthy & M. N. Zald, eds., *Comparative Perspectives on Social Movements: Political Opportunities, Mobilizing Structures, and Cultural Framings*. Cambridge: Cambridge University Press, pp. 152–84.

Kriesi, H. (1999). Movements of the Left, Movements of the Right: Putting the Mobilization of Two New Types of Social Movements into Political Context. In H. Kitschelt, P. Lange, G. Marks & J. D. Stephens, eds., *Continuity and Change in Contemporary Capitalism*. Cambridge: Cambridge University Press, pp. 398–423.

Kriesi, H. (2004). Political Context and Opportunity. In D. A. Snow, S. A. Soule & H. Kriesi, eds., *The Blackwell Companion to Social Movements*. Oxford: Blackwell, pp. 67–90.

Kriesi, H., Koopmans, R., Duyvendak, J. W. & Giugni, M. (1995). *New Social Movements in Western Europe: A Comparative Analysis*. Minneapolis: University of Minnesota Press.

Kriesi, H., Lorenzini, J., Wüest, B. & Häusermann, S., eds. (2020). *Contention in Times of Crisis Recession and Political Protest in Thirty European Countries*. Cambridge: Cambridge University Press.

Marino, B., Martocchia Diodati, N. & Verzichelli, L. (2022). The Personalization of Party Politics in Western Europe (1985–2016): Evidence from an Expert Survey. *Acta Politica*, 57, 571–96.

Marsh, A. (1977). *Protest and Political Consciousness*. London: Sage.

Marsh, A. & Kaase, M. (1979). Background of Political Action. In S. H. Barnes & M. Kaase, eds., *Political Action: Mass Participation in Five Western Democracies*. Beverly Hills, CA: Sage, pp. 97–136.

McAdam, D. (1983). Tactical Innovation and the Pace of Insurgency. *American Sociological Review*, 48(6), 735–54.

McAdam, D. (1999 [1982]). *Political Process and the Development of Black Insurgency, 1930–1970*, 2nd ed. Chicago, IL: University of Chicago Press.

McAdam, D. (2022 [2013]). Tactical Interaction and Innovation. In D. A. Snow, D. della Porta, D. McAdam & B. Klandermans, eds., *The Wiley-Blackwell Encyclopedia of Social and Political Movements*. Oxford: Blackwell, pp. 2133–4.

McAdam, D, & Rucht, D. (1993). The Cross-National Diffusion of Movement Ideas. *Annals of the American Academy of Political and Social Science*, 528, 56–74.

McAdam, D. & Tarrow, S. (2019). The Political Context of Social Movements. In D. A. Snow, S. A. Soule, H. Kriesi & H. J. McCammon, eds., *The Wiley Blackwell Companion to Social Movements*. 2nd ed. Oxford: Wiley Blackwell, pp. 19–42.

McAdam, D., Tarrow, S. & Tilly, C. (1996). To Map Contentious Politics. *Mobilization*, 1(1), 17–34.

McAdam, D., Tarrow, S. & Tilly, C. (2001). *Dynamics of Contention*. Cambridge: Cambridge University Press.

McCarthy, J. D., Britt, D. & Wolfson, M. (1991). The Institutional Channeling of Social Movements by the State in the United States. In P. G. Coy, ed., *Research in Social Movements, Conflicts and Change*. Bingley: JAI Press, pp. 45–76.

McPhail, C. (2022 [2013]). Modular Protest Forms. In D. A. Snow, D. della Porta, D. McAdam & B. Klandermans, eds., *The Wiley-Blackwell Encyclopedia of Social and Political Movements*. Oxford: Blackwell, pp. 1329–34.

Meyer, D. S. & Tarrow, S. (1998). A Movement Society: Contentious Politics for a New Century. In D. S. Meyer & S. Tarrow, eds., *The Social Movement*

Society: Contentious Politics for a New Century. Lanham, MD: Rowman and Littlefield, pp. 1–28.

Micheletti, M. (2002, August 14–17). Individualized Collective Action. Paper for the Nordic Political Science Association's Meeting. Aalborg.

Micheletti, M. (2003). *Political Virtue and Shopping: Individuals, Consumerism, and Collective Action*. New York: Palgrave Macmillan.

Morozov, E. (2011). *The Net Delusion: How Not to Liberate the World*. London: Allen Lane.

Norris, P., ed. (1999). *Critical Citizens: Global Support for Democratic Government*. Oxford: Oxford University Press.

Norris, P. (2002). *Democratic Phoenix: Reinventing Political Activism*. Cambridge: Cambridge University Press.

Norris, P. (2011). *Democratic Deficit: Critical Citizens Revisited*. Cambridge: Cambridge University Press.

Norris, P., Walgrave, S. & Van Aelst, P. (2005). Who Demonstrates? Antistate Rebels, Conventional Participants, or Everyone? *Comparative Politics*, 37(2), 189–205.

O'Toole, T. (2003). Engaging with Young People's Conceptions of the Political. *Children's Geographies*, 1(1), 71–90.

Passy, F. & Monsch, G.-A. (2020). *Contentious Minds: How Talk and Ties Sustain Activism*. Oxford: Oxford University Press.

Pettigrew, T. F. (1996). *How to Think Like a Social Scientist*. New York: HarperCollins.

Pianta, M. (2004). *UN World Summits and Civil Society: The State of the Art. Programme on Civil Society and Social Movements*. Programme Paper Number 18, UNRISD, Geneva.

Putnam, R. D. (2000). *Bowling Alone: The Collapse and Revival of American Community*. New York: Simon & Schuster.

Quaranta, M. (2017). Protest and Contentious Action. *Oxford Research Encyclopedia of Politics*. https://oxfordre.com/politics/view/10.1093/acrefore/9780190228637.001.0001/acrefore-9780190228637-e-225.

Rucht, D. (1998). The Structure and Culture of Collective Protest in Germany since 1950. In D. Meyer & S. Tarrow, eds., *The Social Movement Society: Contentious Politics for a New Century*. Lanham, MD: Rowman and Littlefield, pp. 29–58.

Rucht, D. (2002). The EU as a Target of Political Mobilisation: Is There an Europeanisation of Conflict? In R. Balme, D. Chabanet & V. Wright, eds., *L'action collective en Europe. Collective Action in Europe*. Paris: Presses de Sciences Po, pp. 163–94.

Rucht, D. (2007). The Spread of Protest Politics. In R. J. Dalton & H. D. Klingemann, eds., *The Oxford Handbook of Political Behavior*. Oxford: Oxford University Press, pp. 708–23.

Sartori, G. (1970). Concept Misformation in Comparative Politics. *American Political Science Review*, 64(4), 1033–53.

Schlozman, K. L., Burns, N. E., & Verba, S. (1994). Gender and the Pathways to Participation: The Role of Resources. *Journal of Politics*, 56(4): 963–90.

Schlozman, K., Burns, N., Verba, S., & Donahue, J. (1995). Gender and Citizen Participation: Is There a Different Voice? *American Journal of Political Science*, 39(2), 267–93.

Shorter, E. & Tilly, C. (1974). *Strikes in France*. Cambridge: Cambridge University Press.

Siim, B. (2000). *Gender and Citizenship: Politics and Agency in France, Britain and Denmark*. Cambridge: Cambridge University Press.

Smith, J. & Johnston, H., eds. (2002). *Globalization and Resistance: Transnational Dimensions of Social Movements*. Lanham, MD: Rowman and Littlefield.

Snyder, D. & Kelly, W. R. (1977). Conflict Intensity, Media Sensitivity and the Validity of Newspaper Data. *American Sociological Review*, 42(1), 105–23.

Soysal, Y. N. (1994). *Limits of Cititzenship: Migrants and Postnational Membership in Europe*. Chicago, IL: University of Chicago Press.

Stolle, D. & Micheletti, M. (2013). *Political Consumerism: Global Responsibility in Action*. Cambridge: Cambridge University Press.

Stolle, D., et al. (2005). Politics in the Supermarket: Political Consumerism as a Form of Political Participation. *International Political Science Review/ Revue Internationale de Science Politique*, 26(3), 245–69.

Stover, K. & Cable, S (2017). American Women's Environmental Activism. In H. McCammon, V. Taylor, J. Rege & R. Einwohner, eds., *The Oxford Handbook of US Women's Social Movement Activism*. Oxford: Oxford University Press, pp. 685–707.

Tarrow, S. (1989). *Democracy and Disorder: Protest and Politics in Italy, 1965–1975*. Oxford: Clarendon Press.

Tarrow, S. (1993). Modular Collective Action and the Rise of the Social Movement: Why the French Revolution Was Not Enough. *Politics & Society*, 21(1), 69–90.

Tarrow, S. (2011 [1994]). *Power in Movement: Social Movements and Contentious Politics*, 2nd ed. Cambridge: Cambridge University Press.

Tarrow, S. (2001). *Transnational Politics: Contention and Institutions in International Politics*. Annual Review of Political Science 4, 1–20.

Tarrow, S. (2005). *The New Transnational Contention*. Cambridge: Cambridge University Press.
Tarrow, S. (2012). *Strangers at the Gates: Movements and States in Contentious Politics*. Cambridge: Cambridge University Press.
Tarrow, S. (2022 [2013]). Contentious Politics. In D. A. Snow, D. della Porta, D. McAdam & B. Klandermans, eds., *The Wiley-Blackwell Encyclopedia of Social and Political Movements*. Oxford: Blackwell, pp. 491–4.
Tarrow, S. (2014). Contentious Politics. In D. della Porta & M. Diani, eds., *The Oxford Handbook of Social Movements*. Oxford: Oxford University Press, pp. 86–107.
Taylor, V. (1989). Social Movement Continuity: The Women's Movement in Abeyance. *American Sociological Review*, 54(5), 761–75.
Taylor, W. K. & Tarrow, S. (2024). *Law, Mobilization, and Social Movements*. Cambridge: Cambridge University Press.
Teorell, J., Torcal, M. & Montero, J. R. (2007). Political Participation: Mapping the Terrain. In J. W. van Deth, J. R. Montero & A. Westholm, eds., *Citizenship and Involvement in European Democracies: A Comparative Analysis*. London: Routledge, pp. 334–57.
Teune, S., ed. (2010). *The Transnational Condition: Protest Dynamics in an Entangled Europe*. New York: Berghahn Books.
Theocharis, Y. & van Deth, J. W. (2017). *Political Participation in a Changing World: Conceptual and Empirical Challenges in the Study of Citizen Engagement*. London: Routledge.
Theocharis, Y. & van Deth, J. W. (2018). The Continuous Expansion of Citizen Participation: A New Taxonomy. *European Political Science Review*, 10(1), 139–63.
Tilly, C. (1982). Charivaris, Repertoires and Urban Politics. In J. M. Merriman, ed., *French Cities in the Nineteenth Century*. London: Hutchinson, pp. 73–91.
Tilly, C. (1986). *The Contentious French: Four Centuries of Popular Struggle*. Cambridge, MA: Belknap Press.
Tilly, C. (1995). *Popular Contention in Great Britain, 1758–1834*. Cambridge, MA: Harvard University Press.
Tilly, C. & Tarrow, S. (2015 [2006]). *Contentious Politics*, 2nd ed. Oxford: Oxford University Press.
Topf, R. (1995). Beyond Electoral Participation. In D. Fuchs & H.-D. Klingemann, eds., *Citizens and the State*. Oxford: Oxford University Press, pp. 52–91.
Trottier, D. & Fuchs, C., eds. (2015). *Social Media, Politics and the State: Protests, Revolutions, Riots, Crime and Policing in the Age of Facebook, Twitter and YouTube*. New York: Routledge.

Useem, B. (1998). Breakdown Theories of Collective Action. *Annual Review of Sociology*, 24, 215–38.

Uwe, K. H. R. (1998). Domestic and Supranational Political Opportunities: European Protest in Selected Countries 1980–1995. European Integration online Papers (EIoP) Vol. 2 (1998) N° 5.

Uwe, K. H. R. (1999) United in Opposition? A Cross-National Time-Series Analysis of European Protest in Three Selected Countries, 1980–1995. *Journal of Conflict Resolution*, 43(3), 317–42.

Van Aelst, P. & Walgrave, S. (2001). Who Is That (Wo)man in the Street? From the Normalisation of Protest to the Normalisation of the Protester. *European Journal of Political Research*, 39(4), 461–86.

van Deth, J. W. (2014). A Conceptual Map of Political Participation. *Acta Politica*, 49, 349–67.

Vasi, I. B. & Suh, C. S. (2016). Online Activities, Spatial Proximity, and the Diffusion of the Occupy Wall Street Movement in the United States. *Mobilization*, 21(2), 139–54.

Vassallo, F. (2018). The Evolution of Protest Research: Measures and Approaches. *Political Science and Politics*, 51(1), 67–72.

Verba, S., Nie, N., & Kim, J. (1978). *Participation and Political Equality*. Chicago, IL: University of Chicago Press.

Visser, J. (2012). The Rise and Fall of Industrial Unionism. *Transfer: European Review of Labour and Research*, 18(2), 129–41.

Acknowledgments

We would like to thank the two editors of the Cambridge Elements in Contentious Politics series, David Meyer and Suzanne Staggenborg, as well as an anonymous reviewer for their helpful comments on a previous draft.

Contentious Politics

David S. Meyer
University of California, Irvine

David S. Meyer is Professor of Sociology and Political Science at the University of California, Irvine. He has written extensively on social movements and public policy, mostly in the United States, and is a winner of the John D. McCarthy Award for Lifetime Achievement in the Scholarship of Social Movements and Collective Behavior.

Suzanne Staggenborg
University of Pittsburgh

Suzanne Staggenborg is Professor of Sociology at the University of Pittsburgh. She has studied organizational and political dynamics in a variety of social movements, including the women's movement and the environmental movement, and is a winner of the John D. McCarthy Award for Lifetime Achievement in the Scholarship of Social Movements and Collective Behavior.

About the Series

Cambridge Elements series in Contentious Politics provides an important opportunity to bridge research and communication about the politics of protest across disciplines and between the academy and a broader public. Our focus is on political engagement, disruption, and collective action that extends beyond the boundaries of conventional institutional politics. Social movements, revolutionary campaigns, organized reform efforts, and more or less spontaneous uprisings are the important and interesting developments that animate contemporary politics; we welcome studies and analyses that promote better understanding and dialogue.

Cambridge Elements

Contentious Politics

Elements in the Series

Mobilizing for Abortion Rights in Latin America
Mariela Daby and Mason W. Moseley

Black Networks Matter: The Role of Interracial Contact and Social Media in the 2020 Black Lives Matter Protests
Matthew David Simonson, Ray Block Jr, James N. Druckman, Katherine Ognyanova and David M. J. Lazer

Law, Mobilization, and Social Movements: How Many Masters?
Whitney K. Taylor and Sidney Tarrow

Have Repertoire, Will Travel: Nonviolence as Global Contentious Performance
Selina R. Gallo-Cruz

The Anarchist Turn in Twenty-First Century Leftwing Activism
John Markoff, Hillary Lazar, Benjamin S. Case and Daniel P. Burridge

Sixty Years of Visible Protest in the Disability Struggle for Equality, Justice, and Inclusion
David Pettinicchio

Aggrieved Labor Strikes Back: Inter-sectoral Labor Mobility, Conditionality, and Unrest under IMF Programs
Saliha Metinsoy

The Evolution of Authoritarianism and Contentious Action in Russia
Bogdan Mamaev

Relation-Building and Contained Radicalization in the Gaza Pullout Campaign
Eitan Y. Alimi

Protest Walls: Co-authoring Contentious Repertoires
Yao-Tai Li and Katherine Whitworth

Protest and Policy in the Iraq, Nuclear Freeze and Vietnam Peace Movements
David Cortright

The Transformation of Protest Politics
Marco Giugni and Maria Grasso

A full series listing is available at: www.cambridge.org/ECTP

For EU product safety concerns, contact us at Calle de José Abascal, 56–1°,
28003 Madrid, Spain or eugpsr@cambridge.org.

www.ingramcontent.com/pod-product-compliance
Lightning Source LLC
LaVergne TN
LVHW011856060526
838200LV00054B/4363